ANGER MANAGEMENT FOR PARENTS

THE ULTIMATE GUIDE TO UNDERSTAND YOUR TRIGGERS, STOP LOSING YOUR TEMPER, MASTER YOUR EMOTIONS, AND RAISE CONFIDENT CHILDREN

VIVIAN FOSTER

CONTENTS

A FREE GIFT FOR MY READERS!

Included with your purchase of this book is your free copy of

Kids and Electronics
9 practical strategies to help you manage and limit your children's screen use

Scan the QR code below to receive your free copy:

INTRODUCTION

---

*Anger doesn't solve anything. It builds nothing,
but it can destroy everything.*

— LAWRENCE DOUGLAS WILDER

Around 84% of people in the U.S. are angrier today
than they were a generation ago and these statistics
are echoed elsewhere in the world. In the U.K., for
instance, almost one-third of people polled said they
had a close friend or family member who had a
problem with anger management. Anger can hurt not
only the person experiencing it but also their children.
Sometimes, anger can be abusive.

A study published in the journal *Development and Psychopathology* (Suffren et al, 2021) has revealed that harsh parenting practices that "fall short of serious abuse"(including hitting, shaking, or yelling) cause long-term effects on children's brains, including decreased brain size. Previous studies have already shown that children who experience severe abuse have smaller brain structures that are linked to emotional regulation, anxiety, and depression. There is also a link between harmful behaviors such as bullying, substance abuse, and childhood emotional turmoil.

Anger is a fundamental human emotion that can be constructive instead of destructive when well-managed. When you're a parent—especially a busy one —it almost seems that anger is impossible to control. Take a typical scenario: your child may ask for a toy or gadget during lunch that you have told them they could not play with at mealtimes. Your child may then try various tactics to get what they want: shouting, crying, tugging at your shirt— all in front of family friends. You ask them gently to stop once, twice, three times then you feel like you're going to explode. You grit your teeth, raise your voice to them, or push their hands away from the toy brusquely, and your heart begins to pound. You feel helpless; you wish your child were anything but this strong-willed creature raising their voice back at you, and you feel a deep sense of shame as you notice others around the table taking in the whole fiasco. To make matters worse, you had a horrible morning at work, and all you wanted was to enjoy a delicious meal with loved ones. Why does it seem like everyone else's kids listen to what they say, and why does nobody seem flustered and "out of control" as you feel right now?

When you explode and send your child to their room, and they continue to shout and scream, you can feel like the biggest disappointment on the planet. You try so hard to get it right but as your child gets older, the tension and shouting seem to get worse instead of better. You may also be concerned that these angry episodes are escalating in severity or lasting longer each time. You may feel less and less in control and start to recall your own childhood and the unpleasant episodes you may have experienced with your parents. You wouldn't have dared talk to them like this, raised your voice to them, or resisted when told to pipe down. How did you get to this helpless point in your life and how can you make the switch while there is still time?

In many ways, what fueled my interest in psychology was my own experience with anger. I grew up in a home with little stability. My father was frequently away from home, working on oil rigs in various parts of the U.S. When he was home, he was prone to explosive outbursts of anger, which were always impossible to predict. He could be fine and happy one day, joking around with my older sister and me and poking fun at himself but if we indulged in this humor the next day, we could be faced with a verbal outburst or, worse yet, physical punishment. My mother feared him too and sometimes, to calm his anger, instead of defending us, she would side with him and shout at us too before he got angrier and began punishing us with his belt. I remember crying in my room, feeling demeaned and belittled. The belt hurt but his words hurt more. He would frequently insult us where it hurt the most: insulting our appearance, intelligence, or personality.

Determined to avoid making the same mistakes with my own children and to help heal other victims of anger, I dedicated my life to psychology, which I have been studying for two decades now. Over the past 15 years, I have been almost exclusively dedicated to childhood development and parenting since I know first-hand how much damage growing up in a chaotic environment can cause. While I studied, I also worked on my trauma, and therapy played a key role in helping me dig myself out of the hole I had been hiding in for so many years. Alongside therapy, my studies helped me distance myself from my experience and view everyone

—myself, my father, my mother, and my sister —from afar. When I did so, I was surprised by the deep empathy I felt for everyone involved—including my parents. I knew that if they had the information, skills, and experience I do now, they could have channeled their anger in a far more positive way, using it to effect change instead of succumbing to its destructive power.

I hope to share the many lessons I learned by helping others and by working to change my own perspective. I will start by sharing information on what anger actually is and how it actually has nothing to do with your child. Once you know your triggers and you learn to recognize the signs of anger, you can learn to control your emotions and connect with your loved ones more effectively.

The saddest thing about anger is that when you use it, the important messages you need to express often get lost in fear, shame, guilt, and rejection. Use this emotion wisely, though, and you can really get through to your loved ones and achieve the goals you set. You may need time and patience, but little by little, you will see real change—above all, in the way you process and deal with moments that caused painful outbursts in the past. You will also learn more about the effect that anger management has on your child's future ability to handle and express their anger with their loved ones, colleagues, and acquaintances. When your child is screaming, crying, slamming doors, or refusing to do what you ask, it can be hard to recognize that you are effectively staring at yourself in the mirror. That's right, they could have learned how to deal with feelings like frustration, sadness, and anger—from you.

Love is the answer to everything—above all because it can be a powerful motivator for us to make the changes we need to. The conflict resolution and anger patterns we learn as children can be incredibly hard to unlearn. Moreover, each of us can have our preferred or "natural" way of reacting to the situations that trigger us, and learning to adopt a healthier, more productive strategy can seem counter-intuitive and therefore, too difficult.

Often, however, by making one or more small changes to our behavior, we can change the way we think and feel about the situations that once made us lose our cool. We can also adopt healthy behaviors that help us to reach our goals. Tackling stress proactively can also be of great use since it can improve our mood, help us sleep better, and reduce pain. You may be surprised to learn that anger management isn't centered on stifling tough emotions or simply taking a few deep breaths. It involves taking specific steps that take work, authentic commitment, and consistency. Getting the results you want also involves communicating your wishes effectively—and knowing how to listen is arguably the most fundamental pillar of good communication. By learning how to truly be your child's hero, you can encourage them to embrace and mirror your own healthy, positive energy and to love themselves as much as you love them.

One of the most surprising lessons I learned in my own life was the importance of love—a concept that is so often discussed yet sometimes hard to authentically live by. It is important to know how to show your child love in a way they understand but also to be as kind and compassionate to yourself as you are to them. This will give you a sense of unconditional self-acceptance that will help keep you grounded even in the face of difficult situations. When you know who you are, everyday failures sting less and their power to trigger an outburst is significantly reduced.

In this book, I will be sharing practical tools and strategies to help you prevent tense situations from escalating. These include the traffic light system, which will help you learn the stage of anger you are at so you can lead yourself into a calm state and avoid an angry explosion. By being in tune with the mental and physical signs of anger, knowing your and your child's triggers, practicing effective stress relief techniques, and having an array of useful solutions on deck (as well as an "escape plan"), you can optimize and channel your anger more effectively and enjoy a happier and healthier life.

THE ORIGINS OF ANGER

Anger is an emotion characterized by antagonism toward a person or thing that you feel has deliberately done you wrong. Far from being necessarily negative, it is a basic human emotion and it can be a powerful motivator for change. Anger indicates that our limits have been crossed or disrespected. When we are angry, our heart races, our breathing rate goes up, and our cheeks become a little flushed—these are all signs for ourselves and others that we need to react to defend against a perceived threat.

Anger can be the consequence of feeling vulnerable or fearful of an attack *(Stosny, 2018)*. It is an onslaught against our ego (our perception of who we are in our own eyes and the eyes of others). In order to protect ourselves, we sometimes devalue or demean the person or situation who is posing a subjective threat to our vulnerability. Anger is sometimes expressed verbally, but more often than not, it is noticeable in our body language. When we are angry, we can clench our jaw, close our fists, engage in intense eye contact, or furrow our brows.

WHAT IS THE SOURCE OF ANGER?

Scientists believe that the capacity to feel anger has been hardwired into our brain over a period spanning millions of years (Devlin, 2019). It is rooted in our brain's reward system and is activated when our reality does not meet our expectations. Our reward circuitry triggers activity in the amygdala (the region of the brain that is primarily associated with our emotional processes). Thankfully, another region of the brain— the prefrontal cortex (which is responsible for reasoning and making decisions)—usually keeps our anger in check and stops us from doing something we might regret.

Anger can trigger the body's "fight or flight response," which prepares us to face an enemy or flee from it. When this response is invoked, blood rushes away from the gut toward our muscles and our heart and breathing rates rise (as does our temperature).

The adrenal glands flood the body with stress hormones such as testosterone and adrenaline, preparing us for physical defense. This response was designed to help us in our caveman days when wild animals or foes endangered life and limb. In modern times, however, authentic danger is rare and the "fight or flight response" can trigger a number of problems ranging from anxiety to phobias. It can also make it impossible to reason with another person or to communicate with them in a calm, effective manner.

THE UPSIDE TO ANGER

In addition to helping us defend ourselves against situations where we need to protect ourselves against an enemy or imminent danger, anger has many benefits. One is stress relief. Anger can cause physical and emotional pain and distress, prompting us to do something to remedy these sensations. As we release our tension, the body enters into a calmer state in which it is easier to reason with others and understand our reactions to the person or situation that triggered our anger.

Anger can make us feel less vulnerable and more intent on asserting our limits and demanding that they be respected. Both at work and in our social interactions, this powerful emotion can help us stand up for ourselves, especially when we feel like someone is trying to take advantage of our kindness.

Sometimes, anger can be indicative of an obstacle that is standing in the way of our happiness. When a person or situation frequently or regularly provokes us, it can be a sign that we need to work on relationships, say no more often, or even turn a new page in life—especially when we feel that we are the victims of injustice. In some cases, leaving may not be the answer. Instead, bargaining may be the way to move forward. Anger can be a useful negotiation tool since it can help you stand your ground and state your terms unequivocally.

Often, anger is a way to block out more painful emotions. For instance, if a partner leaves you or you are fired from a job, feeling angry is a way to (at least temporarily) avoid sadness and depression since it enables you to focus your emotions on someone (or something) else.

Being able to feel, identify, and calm anger is also a powerful sign of emotional intelligence. Only those who are self-aware gain positive lessons from even the most painful of emotions. Doing so makes them resilient to life's vicissitudes and enables them to separate their actions and emotions from their identity.

If you think back on your life, there are probably many situations in which healthy expressions of anger were called for. These may have included civil and human rights violations, health inequalities, loneliness, financial problems, and even situations that may have caused you confusion or frustration. The problem with anger never lies in feeling it, but rather, in expressing it in a way that can harm yourself or others. Musician John Mayer hit the nail on the head when he said, "The emotionally intelligent person is skilled in four areas: identifying emotions, using emotions, understanding emotions, and regulating emotions."

THE SYMPATHETIC AND PARASYMPATHETIC SYSTEMS

Anger negatively affects our health when it causes an imbalance between our sympathetic nervous system and our parasympathetic nervous system. The former is responsible for the "fight or flight response" while the parasympathetic system is responsible for maintaining homeostasis or balance. Both systems need to work optimally (similarly to the way a car needs both its accelerator and brakes to function as intended). If you are under chronic stress and you are angry too frequently, it is a sign that your sympathetic and parasympathetic systems are no longer working together harmoniously.

THE HARMFUL EFFECTS OF ANGER

Anger can affect your physical and mental health in many ways, reducing your resistance to disease and setting in motion a plethora of reactions that can promote inflammation, premature aging, and other health problems.

Anger and the Immune System

People who are often angry can fall prey to illness more often than those who are calm. Wounded patients with below-average levels of anger control, for instance, have been found to heal more slowly than those who are more skilled at managing their anger. Numerous studies have also shown that chronically stressful situations weaken immune responses, significantly reducing the body's antibody production when a person is vaccinated against influenza and pneumococcal pneumonia. Positive emotions and guided relaxation, on the other hand, are linked to an improvement of cell-mediated immunity and antibody response to infection.

Anger and the Heart

Anger has a negative impact on many bodily systems, with one study *(European Society of Cardiology, 2014)* finding that outbursts of anger can trigger heart attacks, strokes, and other cardiovascular problems in the two hours immediately following. The risk of a heart attack, for instance, rises nearly five-fold and those who have pre-existing cardiovascular problems can be even more severely affected.

Another study (Duke University Medical Center, 2004) showed that people who tend to be angry and hostile and who have mild to moderate depression produce higher levels of C-reactive protein (which promotes cardiovascular disease and stroke). As stated by researcher Edward Suarez, most people associate heart disease with smoking, sedentarism, high cholesterol, and other factors, but psychological factors such as anger can also have a big impact on one's heart health.

Anger and Lung Power

You may need major lung power to belt out words of hostility, but anger actually speeds up the natural decline in lung power that happens as you age. One study (*BMJ Specialty Journals*, 2006) showed that lung function was significantly lower among male partici-pants who exhibited high levels of anger and hostility.

The authors stated that it would be "hard to find a disease for which emotion or stress plays absolutely no part in symptom severity, frequency, or intensity of flare-ups." Indeed, one study (Wiley-Blackwell, 2010) showed that negative emotions like anger and sadness amplified pain perception in women with and without fibromyalgia.

Anger and General Physical Health

Having negative emotional difficulties is linked to a wide range of medical issues—including headaches, asthma, dermatological eruptions, hypertension, cardiovascular problems, and ulcers (Fernandez & Turk, 1994). Sometimes, these conditions can cause discomfort or pain, which in turn can exacerbate anger. People battling chronic pain, for instance, can internalize their anger, becoming more prone to developing conditions like hypertension. On the other hand, those who lack emotional control may be less prone to hypertension, yet more likely to have coronary heart disease. Anger affects the body in sometimes mysterious ways, and pain, disease, and anger are inexorably linked.

Anger and Your Mental Health

There is a strong link between aggression and anxiety. One study (Chung et al, 2019) found that aggression (indirect aggression such as anger and hostility) is closely related to anxiety. Studies have shown that reactively aggressive children (aged six) are more anxious than their non-aggressive schoolmates. In older children, relational and physical aggression are also considered the strongest predictors of anxiety. Although these studies do not focus on cause-and-effect, they do indicate that aggression often co-occurs with anxiety. People who are subject to anger and hostility, meanwhile, are more likely to have mood disorders such as depression, anxiety, and loneliness.

ANGER AFFECTS OTHERS

Anger can affect the lives of those around you as well since it can cause them stress and be a potential trigger for mental illness. Anger can make you unlikable and it can make others respect you less. This in turn can start a cycle of explosive manifestations of anger that can harm your career and your personal life.

Think of people who are promoted frequently at your workplace. You may notice that one trait most of them have in common is their ability to manage their anger and maintain stability on a day-to-day basis. Sure, they may have bad days and be a little short when they are tired or stressed, but you probably won't catch them slamming the phone down, shouting at subordinates, or superiors, or banging the office door. Most companies have little use for leaders who use angry body language or disrespect themselves or others. After all, this can affect a company's reputation and upset clients.

Anger can also harm your relationships. Regardless of how much your friends and family love you, they have their limits. Unmanaged anger can burn bridges with others because it involves a loss of respect. Your children may also get tired of trying to please you to escape your wrath and as they become teens, they may start spending more time alone in their rooms or indeed looking for a way to escape the tension at home.

HOW DOES ANGER MANIFEST ITSELF?

Anger can be classified into six spectrums (Fernandez, 2008). These are: the direction of anger (which can either be internal or external), the locus of anger (internalizing vs. externalizing), the anger reaction (resistance vs. retaliation), the mode of anger (verbal vs. physical), anger impulsivity (controlled vs. uncontrolled), and the objective of anger (restorative vs. punitive). Knowing how you tend to process and/or express anger is important (so you can be more mindful of aspects such as impulsivity) but it is also vital to observe the dimensions of anger expressed by your loved ones. For instance, you may associate anger with raising your voice and gesticulating but your child may internalize anger, stifling it and masking it only to explode later with the slightest trigger.

TYPES OF ANGER

Researchers (Kapur, 2021) have defined 10 types of anger: assertive, behavioral, chronic, judgmental, overwhelmed, passive-aggressive, retaliatory, self-abusive, verbal, and volatile anger. All have one common consequence: they can have a detrimental effect on a person and their loved ones. They can interfere with personal and professional goals, make it difficult to form and sustain relationships with new people, and stop you from receiving the support and help you need during key moments of your life. Below is a brief description of each anger type:

- *Assertive anger*: Sometimes, anger enables people to bring about positive change, as is the case when it is centered on improving oneself or one's environment. Assertive expressions of anger can motivate others and help overcome fear, stress, and unacceptable or discriminatory actions and behaviors from others. A good example of assertive anger is when a child engages in a dangerous act (such as climbing onto a high wall) you warned them against. By calmly and politely letting them know that this act is wrong, you can actually get through to your child and have a much better chance of your child playing more safely next time. Assertive anger sometimes hits the mark; at other times it doesn't. To avoid getting angry, it can help to focus on using the right strategies patiently and repeatedly, even if they don't give you immediate results.

- *Behavioral anger*: People who engage in behavioral anger may bully, insult, or harass someone else, affecting their physical or mental health or well-being.

- *Chronic anger:* This type of anger is often felt by people who have been through traumatic situations or been the brunt of constant, frequent, or severe anger in their childhood. It may stop individuals from forming healthy, lasting bonds with others.

- *Judgmental anger:* This type of anger can be manifested when a person does not fairly judge the work or behavior of someone else because they are clouded with negative emotions. Underlying this emotion is the feeling that one is better or less than others (in other words, it stems from inequality). Often, it manifests itself in a sense of superiority that can invalidate opinions that differ from one's own.

- **Overwhelmed anger:** When a situation in our lives is beyond our control, it can lead to a sense of frustration and burnout. This can occur when we take on more responsibilities than we can reasonably fulfil and we eventually feel stressed out and frustrated.

- **Passive-aggressive anger:** Anger can manifest itself in the avoidance of confrontation at all costs, only to be expressed in the form of sarcasm, sabotage, mockery, or procrastination. A passive-aggressive co-worker, for instance, may deliberately hold up a project or make themselves impossible to contact.

- **Retaliatory anger:** This type of anger seeks to take vengeance on those who have caused us a perceived wrong. It tends to arise more frequently among family members or close friends who can feel hurt or slighted, leading them to lash out with hurtful words. When two people have this anger disorder, they can aim to "win" an argument by shutting down the other person definitively by weakening their resolve.

- ***Self-abusive anger:*** People with low self-esteem can express this type of anger through negative self-talk, self-harm, substance abuse, and other risky behaviors.

- ***Verbal anger:*** Although often seen as less dangerous than physical manifestations of anger, words can hurt and their damage can last a lifetime. Verbal anger can involve shouting, insults, mocking, bullying, and humiliation. After behaving this way, a person can feel ashamed and guilty but at a loss as to how to make amends.

- ***Volatile anger:*** An extremely harmful anger type that can cause loved ones and colleagues to "tiptoe" around a person, fearing their next outburst.

Identifying different types of anger is important because specific strategies can help in each case. For instance, those who cannot control their outbursts can rely on methods such as controlled breathing when they start to recognize signs such as a faster heart rate or flushed skin. Those who express verbal anger, meanwhile, can hone their conflict resolution skills, learning to use assertive, non-hurtful language to get their point across. When any anger disorder is severe or results in self-harm or abuse toward others, seeking professional help is important because in some cases, explosive and/or constant anger can cause serious physical and/or mental harm to oneself or others.

HOW ANGER AFFECTS YOUR CHILD

Your anger can affect your child and threaten their health and well-being when they are older. A study published in the journal *Developmental Psychology* (Calvete et al, 2015) showed that children who have been exposed to family violence (physical or verbal) at home can grow up to be narcissistic teens who physically or verbally abuse their parents in turn. Other contributors can include a lack of affectionate and positive communication and a lack of quality time with parents.

Another study (Strayer, 2004) found that parents who use induction or reasoning with children and who help their children understand the consequences of their actions ensure that children gain internal regulation and planning skills. They also reduce their children's resentment. By contrast, parenting practices that arbitrarily assert power increase child frustration, indignation, and anger. This situation is made even worse when a parent lacks warmth.

Children of angry parents are less empathetic and they can have problems with social interaction and conflict resolution. They can also experience long-term effects from aggressive or angry behavior from their parents, including a higher risk of depression, spousal abuse, and problems in their professional lives. If you have anger management problems, then simply letting it slide can affect your child and their families for many years to come. It is therefore important to recognize that anger can have serious consequences and that taking proactive steps to manage it is a more-than-worthwhile investment of time and effort.

THE EFFECTS OF SHOUTING

It is funny how people instinctively raise their voice when they are angry—keen, perhaps, to block out others' arguments and force others to truly hear them. Of course, when you yell, you usually achieve exactly the opposite—your child and other loved ones can lose respect for you, "tuning out" to preserve their own peace and well-being. Recent research shows that shouting makes children more aggressive but also makes them feel fearful and insecure. Moreover, when screaming is accompanied by insults or put-downs, it can amount to emotional abuse and many adults still carry the scars of the painful and demeaning comments made to them when they were younger. These comments can come back in a flash, making them relive the incident and affecting their self-confidence.

Shouting can also make children more susceptible to the demands of bullies, since their understanding of healthy limits becomes skewed.

CHILDREN MIRROR THEIR PARENTS' ANGER STYLES

Children who grow up in a home in which their parents shout at each other, call each other names, and mock each other can repeat these behaviors, not only with their parents but also (when they are adults) with their partners and children. It makes sense that a child should repeat the conflict resolution styles they have learned at home. For instance, if they have seen their parents get into heated arguments and one parent usually ends them by leaving the home, slamming the door behind them, then they may adopt heated or avoidant conflict resolution styles in their adulthood.

Children can also build up an aggressive personality to guard themselves against anyone belittling, disrespecting, or yelling at them when they are older. They may adopt bullying behaviors, establishing themselves as someone to fear so that nobody hurts them in turn. Even those who do not bully their peers can use anger to raise their status or authority within an organization or within a group.

WHY DO PARENTS GET SO ANGRY AT THEIR CHILDREN?

All parents get angry at their children and specific circumstances—including working from home, having a high-pressure job, and having to "save" our children from screen addiction—can all push parents past their boiling point. When you have more than one child, meanwhile, having to take part in a conference call or attend to a loved one over the phone can be next-to-impossible when two or more kids are screaming at each other, crying, or pulling toys out of each other's hands. If these scenarios sound all-too-familiar, it's probably because they are the stuff that everyday life is made of, especially when you have children who have yet to learn to reason and control their anger. Of the many jobs you have as a parent, however, arguably the most important one is managing your emotions and giving your children an excellent example to model themselves upon.

Sometimes, we react to our children angrily because they make us feel out of control. If we have a child who is highly sensitive and cries quickly (for instance, when they drop a pencil or if someone momentarily takes a toy they are playing with) then our mind can jump to the worst possible conclusion. In this case, we may think that our child will always be too sensitive to make friends, control themselves in front of teachers, or work successfully with classmates on group projects. You might even conclude that their tantrums reflect on you as a parent and you may blame yourself for not knowing how to help your child reason out. Children can also trigger past memories. They can remind us of a demanding, controlling, or perfectionistic parent, despite the fact that most times, they are simply not old enough to control their emotions. When you begin to feel like your burden is too heavy, pause and understand that these tension-filled moments do not define your relationship with your child. They are fleeting and, if you were to physically measure your child's tantrums to see how long they lasted, you could be surprised to find that they nearly always seem longer than they actually are. Just because your children cry, it does not mean they are complainers. Just because they do not like sharing toys at some point in their lives does not make them selfish. Even if they hit a sibling during a tantrum one day, it does not mean they are physically aggressive.

When you most feel like you are getting parenting all wrong, sit back and remember the saying, "You are much more than the worst thing you've ever done." Extend the generosity of this phrase to your child and take the focus off them. Another useful phrase to keep in mind is contained in the book *Why Won't You Apolo-*

gize? Healing Big Betrayals and Everyday Hurts (Lerner, 2017). The author writes: "If our intention is to have a better relationship, we need to be our best and most mature self, rather than reacting to the other person's reactivity." Lerner adds that some of the other person's (in this case, your child's) complaints may be true since nobody gets everything right all of the time.

EVERYBODY GETS ANGRY, SOMETIMES

Anger is a basic human emotion (Williams, 2017). Neuroscientific research has shown that it has a phylogenetic (evolutionary) origin and that it has contributed to human survival. Anger has a double role: it works inwardly with respect to a pressure we need to overcome or an obstacle we are facing, but it also works outwardly, sometimes creating conflict with others. Basic emotion theory stipulates that anger, like happiness, sadness, and fear, evolved so human beings could handle tasks and challenges.

Anger can be a sign that we are giving too much or even "giving in" to the desires of others with little respect for our own needs or our own self-growth. Sometimes it can appear out of nowhere because we are tired and stressed or because we lack sleep. At other times, it can simmer slowly and eventually cause us to our lid when we feel unappreciated or stripped of our basic rights to rest, evolve, or simply "be."

Because anger is a universal human emotion, there is no way to escape it and as you read on, I hope you will discover that you shouldn't try to—because anger serves its purpose and sometimes, it is the only thing that protects you from giving more than you can.

You cannot avoid anger, but you can control what you do with it. You can recognize it, allow yourself to feel it, yet still make wise decisions about how you express it to others. It is possible to handle anger strategically, pausing and analyzing what the best, most fruitful thing is to say or do. When things get too tense or hot, sometimes, taking time to be alone may be the best gift you can give yourself. One of the most important things you will learn about anger management is that you have access to an array of solutions that you can choose depending on the given situation or person.

Your aim as a parent is to provide a calm, tranquil, clear mirror against which your children can find their own anchor—one that will allow them to keep it together during the most challenging moments of their lives. Keeping your anger in check will allow you to build strong, positive emotional bonds with your child. It will also break the chain of violence, aggression, and loss of control that may have made some parents feel helpless as a child.

Knowing how to manage your anger will boost your child's chances of being a healthy adult and of building a loving and supportive home of their own. You have the ability to learn and apply specific strategies that you can perfect over time. When trying useful techniques, remember to exercise self-compassion and to understand that you may have setbacks.

Keep moving forward until your response to anger is based on a reasoned analysis of the situation and the choice of a specific strategy. It is actually possible to be your most mature self when body and mind try to "trick" you into falling prey to your "fight or flight response." When you are in control of anger, you respond rather than react and that can make all the difference.

2

IS IT REALLY YOUR CHILD'S FAULT?

I f you have frequent clashes with your child, you may find yourself labeling them as "difficult," "argumentative," or "unreasonable." Blaming others when conflict ensues is a way of defending or protecting oneself. By shifting the focus onto our children, we can diminish our responsibility for the escalation of conflict. Of course, the "relief" we get by deflecting responsibility doesn't get us very far, which is why it pays to discover why we are actually angry.

KNOWING WHAT'S CONSIDERED NORMAL BEHAVIOR

Children can be challenging indeed. They can display qualities such as rivalry, whining, an aversion to stick to routines, and mouthiness.

These qualities can be surprising, yet most of them may simply be appropriate to the age of your child (Kadane, 2020). For instance, biting is common in babies and toddlers, preschoolers tend to cry a lot more than school-age children, and competitiveness between siblings peaks between the ages of 10 and 15. Having friends you can trust can be really helpful because they can assure you that their kids, too, cried a lot when they were in kindergarten, or fought over toys or clothing with their siblings, way into their teens. It is normal for children to test their (and your) boundaries and to try to get away with strong-willed behavior sometimes. By adjusting your expectations to what is reasonable for their age, you can feel more at peace and know that many of these situations are passing events you may one day look back at and laugh about. I will cover useful strategies for communicating with children when you feel "put to the test" in Chapter Four.

THE THINGS THAT MAKE YOU SNAP

During your day, you may be subjected to many small and large provocations that can slowly (or very quickly) build up your anger quotient. Research indicates (*The Telegraph*, 2009) that around 79% of people get annoyed easily by little things in life. On average, people become annoyed over three times a day. Around 50% of people surveyed, meanwhile, admitted that they were likely to become "grumpy old people" in their senior years!

You are probably more like these people than you think if, not five minutes after leaving your home and driving onto the highway, you start feeling annoyed by tailgaters, people who refuse to use their signals to change lanes, and those who do not stop when you have the right of way. A 2019 survey (Covington, 2021) showed that 82% of drivers in the U.S. admitted to having road rage or driving aggressively at least once in the previous year, while 42% said they had yelled or cursed loudly at another driver. Reckless driving threatens your life and your family's welfare. It is also selfish and it goes against common ideas of fairness and basic human decency. The possibility of an imminent crash can invoke your "fight or flight" response, making you feel hot under the collar and provoking you to yell something at another driver or speed up to overtake them.

Apart from driving, some of the most common sources of anger include people who eat with their mouths full, rude shop assistants, people who cough without covering their mouths, stepping in dog poop, cold callers, bullying, people who talk loudly on their smartphones, and even slow Internet connections.

You may recall the popular Internet meme of the panda going "berserk" and throwing its computer down aggressively onto its desk. Who hasn't chuckled at that image and more importantly, who can't relate to it?

People who work in a typical nine-to-five job can return to their homes with a lot of accumulated baggage and tension from the office. Indeed, in your work scenario, you could come across people who themselves may be struggling with anger management and may have poor conflict resolution skills. Their frustration, curt responses, and passive-aggressive behavior may make your blood start to simmer. You haven't done anything to them, so why are they taking their frustrations out on you?

As you arrive home and unlock your door, you may receive an effusive greeting from your dog yet your pre-teen child may hardly bat an eye, preferring instead to continue playing a computer game. You enter the kitchen and the dishes are dirty, your youngest child is banging the floor above you with a loud toy, and the doorbell rings but nobody answers it. This can be the straw that breaks the camel's back, so if you feel angry that your child has not bothered to look at you and give you a smile or a hug after a hard day, your feelings are more than understandable.

Although you have a right to be angry about not feeling appreciated and loved at this moment, unleashing your fury on your children, spouse, or the mail carrier isn't an ideal move. The fact that other people in your shoes would explode in a rage does not mean that you should. Now is the precise time for you to muster all of your psychological strength to rise above the situation and react calmly—and yes, sometimes this can seem close to impossible.

Funnily enough, when your partner or children say "Don't take your horrible day with your boss out on me," it can sting and make you even angrier because often, you cannot see the link between the two scenarios and it seems like they are being unfair. It can be very hard to connect your reaction to your child's rudeness to the very first "jerk" who cut you off on the highway that day. Often, people chalk up various successive conflicts to simply having had "a bad day," one in which Murphy's Law seemed to be in full swing. Yet what is more logical—the idea that the universe is conspiring against you, or the possibility that your first conflict made you more prone to engage in a second conflict, then a third, and finally, in the yelling match that occurred when you got home?

Everything is related when it comes to emotions. A bad night's sleep, worry about an upcoming project, or, as Alanis Morisette sang, "a traffic jam when you're already late," can all set you off. Yet your child is not to blame for any of these problems. Your child didn't pass you up for a deserved promotion, nor did they keep you waiting for an hour. They may have had a hard day at school as well and playing a computer game for half an hour or so could be their chosen method to reduce stress.

What if, when you got home, instead of shouting at your child for attention, you gently told them that they had a specific number of minutes left to play and that afterward, you would like them to join you for a walk with the family dog? Did you know that just 10 minutes spent in a green space like a park can significantly lower stress hormone levels (Meredith et al, 2020)? If you live in an urban area or it's cold outside, how does cooking together, reading a great book, or playing a game of Jenga or chess sound? Think of how this short amount of time can instantly transform your day while also providing you with a beautiful opportunity to bond with your child. These simple acts can also teach your child healthy ways to disconnect from stressors when they are older and they, too, have to deal with tension coming simultaneously from various sources.

WHY DO WE TAKE OUR ANGER OUT ON OTHERS?

Psychologists sometimes use the term "kicking the barking dog effect" to describe how people take their anger out on someone other than the actual person that provoked this emotion. The term is based on the following story: "A man who was severely berated by his superior chose to suppress his indignation at being spoken to this way. When he came home and saw his dog barking to greet him, he didn't answer in a friendly manner but rather, kicked his pet with strength." In this example, the boss' humiliating words were a strong provocation and the dog's barking was nothing more than a weak trigger.

In a series of experiments, Liu and colleagues (Liu et al, 2021) found that when the provocation and triggering situations are simultaneous, people tend to show greater aggression toward the trigger. Moreover, people who tend to interpret others' words and actions as hostile (even when they are benign) tend to attribute bad intentions to others and become more aggressive in the face of a trigger.

People who ruminate over anger and who repeatedly tell themselves either positive or negative thoughts about it (for instance, "It does my mind good to go over what happened with my boss," or , "I just can't stop myself from thinking about how badly my boss treated me" also tend to have poorer anger management skills. By running the provocative situation over and over in your head, you keep angry thoughts accessible to your brain and your level of anger increases, as does the risk of aggressive behavior (*Salguero et al, 2020*).

Sometimes, people can get angry at others (usually a "safe person" like a partner or friend) even in the absence of a strong trigger—this is called "displaced anger" and it involves forgetting our responsibilities toward the people who love and trust us. With friends and partners, you may be able to get away with curt or rude responses for a handful of occasions but if your outbursts are frequent and/or severe, you can burn bridges to such an extent that trust may break down completely and love may "leave the building" soon after.

Below are a few examples of displaced anger in action:

- You give a marketing presentation for clients and you are proud of your work, since you have spent many sleepless nights creating a perfect branding strategy for them. They are unenthusiastic about what you have produced and ask you to start from scratch, choosing a logo, fonts, and colors that you know are outdated. That day, you go to lunch with a colleague and you are rude to the servers, yelling at them because they are taking too long to bring your drinks.

- You had lunch with your colleagues and some had too much to drink and started bringing up embarrassing anecdotes from the past that you did not want to discuss in front of everyone. You get home and ask your child three times to do a specific chore and one hour later, they still haven't done it. You scream at them and stand before them, using angry body language to get a response.

- You lose your job and start working from home for a much smaller salary until you can figure out a better way to pay the bills. Your neighbor starts listening to rock music at a loud volume. You run to their home, bang on the door, and angrily tell them to shut up and have some consideration.

All these cases are different but they have two things in common: your disrespect and the likelihood that your behavior has not helped you achieve your goal. The people who are at the receiving end of your tantrum may have issues of their own and they may decide that they are not willing to compromise or make an effort to please someone who has crossed their personal limits. In the case of neighbors you have to be particularly careful because you could start a war that escalates over time and leads to a tense home life. These examples might not reflect your own life experiences but you can always think of instances in which you may have displaced your anger when dealing with your child. By simply identifying these moments, you can be better equipped to handle them the next time around.

WHY ARE YOU TAKING YOUR ANGER OUT ON YOUR KIDS?

Despite being the people we most love in our lives, children can be our most powerful triggers. This is because they may have a greater ability than friends, work colleagues, and acquaintances, to activate a painful feeling or experience from our past; perhaps from when we were children. For instance, if you grew up with an older sibling who used to manipulate you by asking for favors (and your pocket money), only to mock you with their friends, tell you to get out when you wanted to join their friend group, and never share what they purchased with their pocket money, you may be especially triggered when your child is eating a bag of chips and you ask for one and they say no.

It seems like a harmless situation and indeed, your child may be too young to know the importance of sharing, but the hurt can run deep and make you feel as unloved and used as you did as a child.

Sometimes, your child may be very similar to one of your parents. They may have the sardonic sense of humor of one parent, the introversion of another, or a sibling's tendency to argue incessantly. They may enjoy competition, like to have the last word, or need a lot of "me" time while you are a sociable extrovert who would love to spend more time with them. You may have lived through some unhappy situations when you were a child and it can seem like you are reliving them with your children. Some situations can make you feel like you are five years old again—frustrated, vulnerable, and having no way out.

For parents across the globe, some of the most common triggers for anger toward children (Sibonney, 2021) include whining, disrespectful words, being told you are "hated," being physically hurt, spills and damage caused to the home, and siblings shouting at each other. There are specific strategies that you can take in each of these cases. For instance, when children are whining, it helps to take one small moment to exercise self-compassion. Tell yourself that your racing heartbeat-clenched fist and tight jaw are all a result of your body potentially entering "fight or flight mode." Be kind to yourself and when you are ready, calmly tell the child who is whining why they cannot do or have something they want, offering them an alternative activity to take their mind off the source of distress.

More often than not, explaining will not help because your child already is past the point of reasoning at that moment. Some children calm down with a hug and attention from their parents. Others whine more when you attempt to soothe them, but react better to distraction. Yet others cry and complain simply because they are tired and need a nap. Judge the situation and ask yourself if what your child is asking is reasonable. If it is not, don't give in to their demands just to quiet them down. This will only teach them that whining and screaming are good ways to get what they want. Try to calmly ignore further requests and if necessary, gently invite them to go to their "quiet place," where they can have a sulk but eventually calm down and join you for a big hug and quality time. When your child has regained control, praise them (Nemours Kids Health, n.d.), saying something like, "I really liked the way you calmed yourself down."

If your child is being disrespectful, you can try putting yourself in their shoes, letting them know that you understand they may not want to do something (for instance, their homework) but that you are there to help them out if they need you. You can tell them something like, "okay, I understand your homework today is hard so let's focus on how you can fix the issue. Can you look for help online? Is there a free Khan Academy tutorial on the subject? Can you send a message to a schoolmate and ask if they know tips for solving that difficult trigonometry question?"

Try to react calmly to painful words ("I hate you" or "I love Daddy more"). They are just your child's way of expressing their frustration because they can't be "boss." Instead of getting into a power struggle with them, when they have calmed down a bit, let them know that your love for them is unconditional. Much later, you can even have a talk and ask them why they said they hated you. They might answer something like "Because you didn't let me stay on my computer." You can then explain that if you let them play too long, they wouldn't manage to fulfil all their duties or sleep on time and that they would be tired the next day. Talking about it afterward calmly and with smiles and hugs is a great way to hold your child accountable for the things they say and to perhaps help them to think twice before saying hurtful words too often in the future.

If your child unwittingly hurts you (toddlers can sometimes headbutt parents unintentionally or scratch them by mistake), try to teach them how to maintain healthy body space. When siblings fight, make safety a priority and encourage each child to enjoy a little "quiet time," bringing them together later to apologize and try to find a solution to their argument.

Finally, if a child unintentionally spills food or breaks a household item, by all means, avoid yelling at them. If a parent yelled at you for breaking a plate or glass in your childhood, then you know how small and helpless it made you feel. Sensitive children can become insecure if parents judge them too harshly. Ask them to help you pick up what has been spilled or to help you fix (or repaint, or glue) an item they have broken. Teach them useful techniques that will avoid spillage in the future (everything from how to pour water into a water bottle to how to eat a bowl of soup).

In all these cases, if you should occasionally lose your cool, hone the art of self-compassion (self-kindness). **A PLOS ONE** study (Ferrari et al, 2018) found that self compassion can be an important buffer against perfectionism. It can stop people from falling into the trap of being over-critical and over-concerned about making mistakes. Self-compassion can also help you "roll with life's punches," facing everyday stressors with grace instead of ruminating or negative events, criticizing yourself, and exaggerating the gravity of problems. In another study (Leary et al, 2007) scientists found that "self-compassion leads people to acknowledge their role in negative events without feeling overwhelmed with negative emotions." In fact, being as kind to your- self as you would to others can be even more beneficial than having self-esteem, because self-compassion is unconditional while self-confidence is based on achievements.

IS IT REALLY YOUR CHILD'S FAULT?

It may seem as though a little child is "sabotaging" us when they seem like they are using every trick in the book to get away with behaviors we don't condone. If you feel that your child has really pushed your buttons on a given day, you may feel extremely frustrated. You may ask yourself, "How did I just let a little three-year- old 'get the better of me' and 'make me' lose my resolve to stay calm?"

Your child can seem particularly "able" at making you explode but in fact, the secret to staying calm does not lie within them. You can spend all their childhood trying to make them quietly conform to your every request but you cannot really change their personality. All children have unique character traits, thoughts, and emotions.

They cry and scream because they are deeply upset about something. As their brain has not yet developed to the point in which they are capable of reasoning between appropriate and inappropriate ways to get what they want, why not be a guide instead of a person who points the fingers at them and blames them for mismanaged anger?

AVOID LABELING YOUR CHILD

Just because your child hit another kid one day at school, it does not mean they are "aggressive." If they cried when they fell while playing football at school, it does not mean they are "depressed." If they like to reason with you and discuss rules or "kids' contracts" before agreeing to terms, it does not mean that they are "difficult." Before placing any label on your child, take note. Research (Pidgeon & Sanders, 2009) has shown that when parents attribute child misbehavior to internal, stable characteristics in the child, they are more likely to become angry and respond negatively to their children. They can also be more explosive when they attribute intent and blame to their kids.

Displacing anger doesn't work when you're dealing with children; it only intensifies the problem. Pidgeon and colleagues found that clinically angry mothers who are at risk of maltreating their children also report being depressed, stressed, and anxious.

It is therefore vital for those experiencing this type of anger to receive professional therapy with a focus on identifying and adapting the way they think, feel, and behave.

CHILDREN ARE VULNERABLE

Some scientists (Piantadosi & Kidd, 2016) argue that human beings have evolved to become the intelligent beings that they are, because human infants are so helpless. In other words, because human brains need a long time to mature and grow, once the process is complete, the result is greater intelligence. The fact that children's brains are developing and are so vulnerable to the input they receive is an important reason why you should be patient, kind, and calm when dealing with them.

A study published in the journal Current Biology (McCrory et al, 2011) showed that the brains of children who are exposed to family anger become increasingly "tuned" to process additional sources of threat. They become more "reactive" (more ready to respond to a perceived threat). Although being in tune to threats can help them respond in the short-term, it may also pose "a neurobiological risk factor" that increases their chances of developing anxiety and other mental conditions when they are older. In the study, children who had been exposed to violence at home had different brain responses to angry and sad faces. When they viewed images of angry people, they showed increased activity in the brain regions involved in detecting stress and anticipating pain. The study is just one of many that show how important it is to take violence and aggression at home seriously. When it comes to our children, the damage of aggression and anger cannot be undone.

CUTTING KIDS SOME SLACK

It is important to reduce your own sources of stress but also to ensure that your kids are not taking on more than they can chew. If you feel like you are constantly playing chauffeur, driving your children from activity to activity, chances are, your children may feel equally overwhelmed. When formulating your child's extra- curricular program, try to obtain their input when it comes to choosing classes and activities, so they have a smaller yet more enjoyable schedule to fulfil. You may find that, if your child is busy with out-of-school activities five times a week, cutting it back to twice weekly may be a big sigh of relief for everyone.

As stated by Boston College researcher, Peter Gray (Gray, 2011), "Children are designed, by natural selection, to play." However, the past five decades have seen a big decline in the opportunities children have to indulge in unstructured outdoor play. The National Recreation and Park Association reports, for instance, that children today devote only four to seven minutes a day to unstructured outdoor play per day, yet can spend seven and a half hours in front of an electronic screen. Yet nature is a healer. It reduces stress, helps kids hone their strength and flexibility, encourages social interaction, boosts self-confidence, and enhances concentration and focus.

A bit of rough-and-tumble play is also important, as is allowing children to explore their natural surroundings independently, test their limits, and formulate useful strategies for dealing with potential danger. All these activities help the child develop a more rounded personality which will aid them enormously in their adult life to deal with life's problems successfully.

THE SURPRISING BENEFITS OF FREE PLAY

Parents often see child's play as a way for kids to let off steam and make gains in strength and flexibility, but unstructured play has a host of additional benefits (Ian- nelli, 2021). The American Academy of Pediatrics high- lights the following gains:

- Play enhances children's creativity and enables their imagination to flow freely.

- It invites them to explore the world around them and discover the many hidden gems that await them in the Great Outdoors.

- Play enhances social interaction and teaches kids valuable lessons about the importance of teamwork, assertiveness, and conflict resolution.

- It boosts a child's ability to adapt to new challenges at school, sparks their interest in learning, and hones their problem-solving skills.

- When indulging in play, children also learn the importance of self-regulation; that is, they learn how to monitor their thoughts, feelings and behaviors.

Peter Gray warns that a lack of play affects emotional development, leading to a rise in anxiety, depression, and attention and self-control issues. He adds that without play, young people fail to acquire the social and emotional skills that they need for healthy psychological development.

REDUCING THE POWER OF EXTERNAL EVENTS TO MAKE YOU ANGRY

Because provocative situations and individuals can result in innocent people "triggering" your anger later, you should utilize strategies that will help cut them out of your relationship with your child. One important strategy involves taking proactive steps to properly disconnect from work. There are many ways in which to do this, one of which is to strictly avoid reading work emails after you have left the office or once your official workday has ended. Another is to avoid going over your difficult day in the car on the way home. Make an effort to fill your mind with productive thoughts. Start out by doing a few breathing exercises. Apps like *Breathe, Calm,* and *Headspace* are a great start. Open *Breathe* and simply take part in a five-minute controlled breathing session. Doing so will not only eliminate stress but also help your brain create new connections (Trinity College Dublin, 2018). Breathing affects the levels of noradrenaline (a natural chemical messenger that is released when we are curious, challenged, or focused).

Another important way to disconnect from work is to be ultra-efficient when you are there. As much as you need the odd distraction, avoid wasting time on apps and websites that can stop you from achieving a set number of goals on a given day.

Check out website blockers like *Freedom* for Mac or Windows, *StayFocused*, *Limit*, and many more that can help you avoid the temptation of addictive sites.

Finally, make a list of all pending tasks you need to complete the next day and leave it on your desk. This way, you won't be running through them when you are driving or commuting back home. If possible, don't make home and work your only two destinations. Make time for hobbies, exercise, and friends. Try keeping many bottles full (friendship, family, interests) instead of making your children the sole focus of your interest. By doing so, you can avoid putting all your energy (both positive and negative) into your children and be a happier, more rounded parent. Your kids will look up to you as a shining example of someone who knows how to achieve a good work-life balance.

RELEASING BLOCKED EMOTIONS

In addition to disconnecting from work, get rid of blocked or repressed emotions to avoid burnout and imbalance (Ciolek, 2018). There are three fundamental steps to processing emotional energy. The first is self-awareness: being aware of the array of emotions and sensations we can feel (ranging from hunger to anxiety, sadness to anger).

Mindfulness training and meditation can help you be more in tune with physical and mental signs of stress. In mindfulness meditation, the aim isn't to repress or "defeat" difficult emotions, but rather, to recognize and accept them, knowing that they do not define you and that they are, like most emotions, fleeting and cyclical. When you are cognitively aware that you are feeling stressed or tired, you can be more aware of the way in which you interact with others. You can also take steps to correct imbalances and reduce the power that triggers have over you.

The next step is to express how you feel—something you can do by keeping a journal, embracing a creative pursuit, or taking up a hobby like photography. Writing can be particularly useful because you can use a journal to track your progress and identify the specific situations that caused you to become angry or engage in subsequent conflicts. You can also study how you reacted on different days, list different strategies you wish to utilize when you feel provoked, and see if you are making progress.

Self-care is the last key step to greater balance and emotional release. Treat yourself to something that leaves you in a better state than you were before it. If the thought of sitting in a movie theatre with a box of popcorn appeals, call a friend and catch a film you have been waiting to see. If you love the peace and calm that nature brings, organize a short camping getaway or simply take a walk through a verdant forest area. If music floats your boat, treat yourself to a musical afternoon, giving yourself the time to listen to an album you love. It's all about treating yourself with care and compassion. The old adage is true—it is impossible to give others your best self if you feel tired, frustrated, or uncared for. Life is challenging and some days are better than others but by caring for yourself consistently, you can stop frustrations from being redirected at your child. Rather, you can be a helpful guide who knows they are still learning how to be their best selves—as we all are.

3

DON'T LET YOUR EMOTIONS CONTROL YOU

A a parent, you have the right to lay down ground rules, establish a routine for children, and ensure they comply with schoolwork and other responsibilities. However, if you really want to see a positive change in them, start with yourself. Making changes to how you think, feel, or behave will not necessarily elicit the response you seek from your children immediately. However, it will enable you to negotiate tough situations more effectively by relying on optimal anger management and conflict resolution tools. Working on yourself is hard—it took an entire childhood and much of your adulthood to become who you are today so give yourself the time you need to unlearn damaging patterns and replace them with effective ones.

It may take weeks or months to "unlearn" harmful techniques and experiment with different strategies until you find the combination that works for you, and you may suffer setbacks along the way. For instance, things may seem much more peaceful at home once you start regulating your emotions and changing your responses but, just when you start resting on your laurels, a fight may ensue and you may find it difficult to control your anger. Progress nearly always involves a few setbacks. On some days, it can seem like you are going one step forward and two steps back. On others, you can feel like you have made big advances. Before learning how to avoid falling prey to negative emotions, you need to fully understand them: how they arise, what their aim is, and why repressing them is the worst thing you can do.

THE IMPORTANCE OF EMOTIONAL EXPRESSION

Keeping emotions bottled up can affect both your quality and quantity of life. One study (Chapman et al, 2013) found that emotional suppression carries a higher risk of an earlier death—including death from cancer. Scientists have found that there are many reasons why keeping emotions inside can be so harmful to health—including the link between poor emotional expression and the adoption of unhealthy behaviors such as smoking and overeating. Secondly, there is a clear connection between suppressing one's emotions and having more frequent, intense emotional reactions. When you lock your feelings inside, an array of physiological reactions can follow, some of which are linked to a higher likelihood of chronic disease (such as heart disease) and death.

Emotional suppression can also affect your mental health and well-being. One study (Lazarus, 1966) asked participants to watch an evocative film. One group of participants was asked to suppress their emotions and the other to express them. Results showed that the group who hid their emotions experienced negative emotions to a higher degree than those who freely expressed them. Suppression is also linked to anxiety and post-traumatic stress disorder (PTSD). Scientists have found that when you suppress your emotions, you dampen positive emotional experiences too, thereby increasing the chances of depression.

EMOTIONAL REGULATION VS. AGGRESSION

Effective emotional regulation involves managing and responding to emotional experiences in a productive manner. Most of us use an array of strategies in emotional regulation, some of which are positive for our physical and mental health and others which are not *(Rolston & Lloyd-Richardson, n.d.)*. Healthy strategies include going to therapy, taking part in yoga or mindfulness meditation classes, making quality sleep a priority, being aware of signs that you need a break, and paying attention to negative thoughts and sensations that arise before you start feeling angry. Unhealthy strategies, on the other hand, include self-harm, completely avoiding conflicts, becoming addicted to social media, substance abuse, and being aggressive toward others.

A situation is not difficult or easy per se; it is the way that we interpret it that makes it so. Take the following scenario: You are at your office and you go to a colleague's desk to discuss the progress of a project. Afterward, you chat for a couple of minutes about each other's families and personal projects and you notice your superior sigh and get up, heading for the bathroom and slamming the door behind them.

You then experience a set of rapid-fire emotions (such as indignation, fear, disappointment) and you start assigning several thoughts about what has just happened. "Did the boss get angry because we were talking?" "Why didn't she ask us to speak more silently if we were bothering her?" "I wonder if she'll tell (a bigger) boss that we were wasting time." "Maybe she was just tired and she got up angrily because she's mad at something she just read on her screen." All these thoughts can then give rise to emotions (fear, anger, insecurity) and you may have a strong desire to suppress these. As you catch the train home you may start to ruminate on the event and worry.

UNDERSTANDING THE LINK BETWEEN YOUR THOUGHTS, EMOTIONS, AND FEELINGS

No single therapy works equally for everyone but one that is widely used in anger management is cognitive behavioral therapy (CBT), which is centered on the relationship between our thoughts, feelings, and behaviors. The therapist aims to increase their client's self-awareness so they can break the negative cycle of emotional dysregulation. Of course, you can also ask yourself important questions that can enable you to work on this goal. Rolston suggests asking yourself a series of questions, including:

- Which thoughts trigger the most difficult emotions for you?
- Which emotions are the hardest for you to feel (and which are the easiest)?
- What behaviors do you engage in when you need to calm yourself down?
- Which of the above behaviors are healthy or

conducive to greater health and happiness in the long term?

- What beliefs about life, people, or yourself perpetuate negative thought cycles?

- What thoughts and beliefs tend to make you feel more positive and more in control of difficult situations?

CBT can be very fruitful when it is approached with commitment and a true desire to change. One of the most fascinating things about it is that it may start by a person changing just one behavior and noticing how doing so can have a profound effect on how they feel or think about a situation. Because what "works" to calm you down is so personal, it is definitely worth writing or listing these positive strategies so you can think of how they may be applicable in more than one circumstance. For instance, if when you are stressed from work, a yoga or meditation session makes you feel as good as new but when you fight with your spouse you get so stressed out that you reach for a pack of cigarettes or a glass of alcohol, you might consider trying meditation the next time you have an argument with your loved one.

If you continue to use harmful coping mechanisms, it can injure your sense of confidence in your ability to behave calmly in the face of provocation and triggers.

This is because when you indulge in harmful behaviors to avoid a negative emotion, you can feel ashamed and guilty about doing so. Shame and guilt, in turn, can prompt you to once again seek escape in harmful coping mechanisms. The cycle usually begins (Chapman et al, 2006) with a triggering event (for instance, a shouting match with your child), followed by emotions (sadness, anger, frustration), then a moment of "high arousal," then a self-sabotaging behavior, and finally, relief. The next time a triggering event happens, the cycle starts all over again.

BEING PROACTIVE INSTEAD OF REACTIVE

In addition to listing your personal strategies for dealing with difficult emotions, it is worth reviewing them and thinking of other situations in which one or more of these strategies could be useful. You may also find it helpful to use the "traffic light system" for anger management. One of the best things about this method is that it can work for children as well as adults, so you can also teach it to your kids. The steps are as follows

▶ **Red Light:**

Identify the negative feeling you are experiencing at a given moment. It could be fear, disappointment, jealousy, sadness, frustration.

If you are finding it hard to identify the emotion, observe the way your body is reacting. If you are furrowing your brow, sweating, glaring, or feeling hot around the ears and neck, you could be angry. If you are trying to make yourself physically small, notice that your heart rate has increased, or breathe fast and shallowly, it could be because you are scared. Identifying emotions may be difficult at first but simply pausing to do so is already an important recognition that something is not quite right and needs reappraisal.

▶ Yellow Light:

Think about the situation that caused you to feel angry, sad, or otherwise negative. Think about what judgmental or negative thing you may have said to yourself to make things worse. Thoughts like "He said hello to everyone except me because he hates me," "My boss frowned when he was listening to my presentation because he wants to fire me," or "She didn't call me on my birthday. She's a bad friend and does not care for me" are typical self-sabotaging thoughts that can be a stronger trigger than they need to be.

Next, come up with an explanation for the situation so you can reinterpret and relabel what you experienced more positively. This is called "reframing the meaning" of the event.

Thus, you could now decide you feel "relieved," "grateful," or "forgiving." The latter is particularly useful when someone hurts you (for instance by forgetting an important day like a birthday or anniversary) without intention.

Different situations may prompt the use of different types of "frames." Life coach and mind mapper, Adam Sicinski (Sicinski, 2018) suggests using a wide array of frames, including:

- Outcome frames—which involve focusing on what you want to achieve so you can direct your emotions, thoughts, and actions in a particular direction.

- "As if" frames—pretending your goal scenario is achieved. You might, for instance, imagine that you stay calm and focused in the face of anger. Simply doing so will put you in a better frame of mind and help you overcome your obstacles.

- Time frames—giving yourself a specific time in which to solve your issue.

- Metaphorical reframes—using metaphors to see your situation in a clearer light.

- Positive intention frames—trying to see good intentions or sound reasons behind specific behaviors.

- Importance reframes—focusing on only one

important thing instead of on everything that was said and done.

- Perspective reframes—thinking of how the other person might be viewing the conflict between you, for instance.
- Alternate choice reframes—How many other ways of solving this issue are there, other than the one you have chosen? Could any be of potential interest?
- Humor reframes—making fun of yourself or the situation.

▶ **Green Light:**

Relish in the new, more positive emotion you are feeling. Allow yourself a little time to feel happy and proud of your accomplishment as well, since you have managed to dramatically reduce the severity of a situation.

WHAT STRATEGIES DO EMOTIONALLY INTELLIGENT PEOPLE USE TO EXPRESS EMOTIONS HEALTHILY?

The traffic light system will stand you in good stead when a provocative situation threatens to start up your "fight or flight" response but there are many additional strategies that can help you become a more emotionally intelligent person. The influential publication, *The Emotionally Intelligent Manager* (Caruso & Salovey, 2004), identifies four key skills that are key to emotional intelligence:

- Identifying your feelings and those of others.

- Using these feelings to guide your thinking and reasoning.

- Understanding that feelings are not permanent; they can change, sometimes dramatically, with the passage of time or changes in circumstances.

- Being open to data about feelings and incorporating them into your reasoning and actions.

The next time you receive an angry email, instead of answering quickly, typing at lightning speed, stop to think and ask yourself: "What emotion am I feeling?" This small pause in itself can start you on a path to greater mindfulness and enable you to respond more effectively.

Emotional intelligence also involves being smart enough to seek feedback from friends and family. When you tell a friend about a problem or a conflict you are having, don't expect them to simply accept everything you say.

Be open to their interpretations of an event, especially if they can help you frame things more positively or suggest new behaviors or strategies. Take time to ask them for information about how you deal with them when a difficult situation arises. Be open and broach the subject with humor and warmth so they can be honest. Try to apply what they have told you to improve your communication style with them and other people.

Be ready to give yourself a "time out" period when you feel overwhelmed instead of confronting someone immediately. Sit back and try to understand what made them speak to you in a way that made you feel unheard, uncared for, or disrespected. Empathy is a key strategy for depersonalizing situations and understanding that everyone else in your life can have a bad day, feel tired, or be battling problems that can make them respond less amicably than they would under normal circumstances. Finally, know that all progress takes time and involves little setbacks. Stay positive about your ability to pause and rethink situations, even if things don't work out perfectly the first time around.

POSITIVE WAYS TO EXPRESS YOUR EMOTIONS

On a day-to-day basis, think of the many ways that you can express your emotions clearly and in a way that is well-received by others. These can include listening to others (to help build empathy), giving yourself positive messages every day, taking care of your spiritual self, reducing the number of noisy distractions around you, forgiving others for unintentionally hurting or bothering you, accepting things about your life you cannot change, aiming to live intentionally in the present moment (instead of regretting things about the past or worrying about the future), trying a new activity or hobby, embarking on an adventure, taking part in visual arts classes, and simply being grateful for all the good things you have. As you can see, there are so many available choices and more often than not, you will find that relying on more than one of them can help keep you more centered and positive.

DIFFERENT STRATEGIES FOR DIFFERENT EMOTIONS

Sometimes, negative emotions call for a different type of action. For instance, if you are deeply sad and this feeling stops you from carrying out your daily tasks, it could signal depression—a condition that should be diagnosed and treated by a professional. If you are scared of something (for instance, if you are scared of flying and you have a flight to take in a couple of days), then finding a distraction such as writing a blog post or sketching still life can pull you out of an anxious or fearful state. If you are disgusted with someone, empathy can help you gain a new perspective on why they let themselves and others down. If you are fuming with anger, it can help to get yourself out of a heated situation by going for a walk in a green area, listening to music, or meeting a friend for lunch. Mindful activities in particular are powerful stress busters.

MAKING POSITIVE BEHAVIORAL CHANGES

I spoke earlier about CBT and its focus on the inexorable relationship between thoughts, emotions, and behaviors. As mentioned, making even one small change in either of these three areas can have a profound effect on the other two. In other words, by behaving in a more productive, reasoned manner (even if you may have doubts about it), you may find that you achieve surprisingly good results. You may then feel happier about a situation and also think about it more positively.

If you keep a journal, write down a few positive behavioral changes you have decided to make. After you have tried them out, record your results. Try each behavior more than once, because its success may very much depend on a myriad of delicate circumstances that won't necessarily be present each time. Also, you may find that some behaviors (for instance, using humor to deflect tension during an argument with your children) work better with some people than with others. Your journal is testimony to how hard you are working to make a change and it is also a kind of "investigation" into the strategies and tactics that produce the best results.

Positive behaviors are very personal since we all have our preferences, values, and beliefs. Just a few that have been shown in studies to benefit the vast majority of people include social interaction (smiling, making eye contact, and conversing with others), practicing assertive body language, listening to music that lifts your spirits, hugging a loved one, and acting out a happy movement (such as skipping, dancing, and hopping). The latter is the perfect instance of a behavior that can almost instantly affect one's mood. It is difficult to carry this activity out without laughing and making others laugh.

Another activity involves laughing out loud—even if nobody has made a funny joke. This activity is particularly enjoyable when carried out with others as what starts as "fake laughter" soon transforms into authentic belly laughs that sometimes give rise to tears of joy. Numerous studies have shown that laughter has a bevy of benefits for your health. It freezes the "fight or flight" response, reduces tension, boosts personal satisfaction, and lifts the mood. It has pretty impressive physiological benefits as well since it is a known immunity booster and pain reliever.

▶ Mood Journaling

Journaling is a popular activity for those who like to express themselves through the written word. It has many benefits, with research showing that it makes our sadness, anger, and pain less intense (University of California-Los Angeles, 2007). This can be attributed to the fact that writing your thoughts and emotions down is inherently mindful. The researchers found that mindfulness boosted activity in the part of the brain involved in reasoning and lowered activation of the brain's emotional center.

When it comes to anger, keeping a mood journal (a journal that focuses specifically on emotions) can be particularly useful (Garone, 2020) for your mental health.

To start your journal, write down the following column titles in your book:

- The name of the emotion felt.
- What caused you to feel it.
- What behaviors or actions the emotion itself caused you to take.
- Is this emotion appropriate to the situation?
- Does this situation or painful/distressful emotion require solving and if so, what practical steps can you take to achieve this goal?

Your journal might look something like this:

The name of the emotion felt	What caused me to feel it	The behaviours or actions the emotion caused me to take	Is this emotion appropriate to the situation?	If this situation/emotion requires solving, what practical steps can I take to achieve this goal?

Filling in these columns can boost your self-awareness regarding aspects such as the emotions that most often get you down, how frequently you are having angry outbursts, and which practical steps are most successful. It can also highlight areas of your life that need prioritization. If you notice, for instance, that you have had very strong or sustained outbursts multiple times each week, you may decide to opt for professional counseling.

Journaling can surprise you, because although your main concern is anger, you may notice that you have other frequent emotions—including worry, fear, and sadness— which could indicate that you have anxiety or depression.

The ultimate aim of journaling is to discover things you may not have consciously been aware of, to learn your main triggers, and to rate the success of different anger management strategies. To make the most of your journaling experience, try to write every evening or as often as you can. Make it easy and appealing by designating a quiet, appealing space for this task. You can keep your journal to yourself, but showing it to a trusted friend or family member can also be a starting point for a discussion on how you deal with anger and allow you to feel more in control of this emotion.

▶ Giving Yourself Time and Space

Life throws a lot of curveballs at you and even when it all seems pretty routine, you may have various obligations pushing you in all directions—your responsibilities to your team, spouse, parents, children, and friends. In order to stay sane and give yourself the gift of well-being, a little "me time" is vital. Time is the greatest luxury and time is money, so where can you find a little more of this precious commodity?

Once again, mindfulness is key, as is sitting down and taking notes. Try to keep a digital schedule that reveals how much time you are spending on each key aspect of your life. This will help you avoid wasting time on unimportant things so you can pencil in a little valuable time for yourself. When doing so, give yourself a little longer than the time you originally envisioned. Sometimes, things like road traffic, calls, and other interruptions can shorten the time you can dedicate to your chosen activity.

Looking back at your schedule will also clearly show the events, meetings, calls, and chats you probably should have said "no" to. Saying "no" can be difficult if you are a "people pleaser" or you are an empath. However, it pays to be mindful of how you spend your free time, since taking care of your own health and well-being is as important as being a giving parent, partner or spouse, worker, and friend.

▶ Turning the Spotlight Back on Your Children

Your anger affects your children because they respond emotionally to the input they receive from you. All humans react to the emotions, words, and other messages but this reaction is even stronger in children because they are still going through many vital stages of development. Your child may be exposed to various types of anger in the home: sudden anger (outbursts which occur when you feel trapped or triggered), settled and deliberate anger (which is a response to deliberate harm or a response to perceived unfairness or violations of your rights), and dispositional anger (which is more like a permanent trait or habit that is usually described as irritability, grumpiness, or crabbiness). Anger can be open or concealed by other behaviors. A child can suffer the effects of anger even when it is directed at someone else (for instance, their sibling or your partner or spouse).

Previously, we mentioned the many ways in which anger can harm your child's health, well-being, and future relationships. There is one more effect that uncontrolled anger can have: it can affect your child's ability to interpret their emotions (Capriola, n.d.). This, in turn, hampers their ability to exercise emotional intelligence and practice useful anger management skills.

As parents, it always pays to ask ourselves a few questions to keep ourselves in check (after all, nobody else is going to do it for us). Key questions to ask include:

- Are you talking about adult matters with your spouse (involving topics like money, sex, family conflicts, and the like) in private or are your children listening to words that they should, perhaps, be shielded from?
- Do you and your spouse communicate in a loving, respectful manner (remember, your child will mirror what he or she sees)?
- Do you try to teach your child important lessons when they do something wrong or do you direct your anger at them, directly or indirectly? When you direct anger at a child, they can close off and stop listening to the words you are saying. Indirect anger, meanwhile, can lead to the adoption of harmful conflict resolution strategies. An example of indirect anger is when you usually deal with tough situations at home by sending them to their room. This may promote distancing behaviors from your child when they are older.

When you keep the focus on your child and always keep their well-being in mind, you can stop yourself before taking their behavior personally. If your child is having a problem, try to soothe them and once they are more relaxed, ask them questions. By conversing with them and giving them quality time, you may be surprised to discover that your child is acting up because they are being bullied at school or because they are afraid to sleep in the dark. Your child's anger can reveal vital information that requires action.

Promote loving feelings and kindness at home and take the time to ask your child why they were angry earlier in the day, or the night before. Don't let the opportunity go by to make small or big changes that your child needs. For instance, if your child is scared of the dark, a simple night light can battle the blues and prevent many a night of crying, worry, and anger.

Let Other Readers Know that Anger Can Be A Powerful Ally Instead of an Enemy

*"Sharing our truths can provide the opportunity for great healing." — **Kristen Noel***

Earlier in this book, I mentioned that few things can make a parent feel like such a big failure as anger. You know the score. You've promised yourself (and your family) time and time again to communicate more calmly. No more shouts, no more threats, no more regrets after the storm.

Yet time and time again, there seem to be situations that are simply "beyond your control." Imagine this scenario. You walk in the door after a hectic day at work. Your youngest child has strewn things all over the floor, your partner is screaming, and your older kids are pulling the TV remote out of each other's hands. You can't help but yell a "Everyone to their room!" without even stopping to ask about what has happened in every situation.

You're human, and anger can sometimes "win." But it doesn't have to all the time. By now, you know more about the origins of anger. You know that when you let your emotions take the wheel, you almost automatically take your emotions out on the people you love. You have also discovered how tools like assertive communication can turn things around, so your anger empowers you to achieve a healthy outcome.

You would be surprised to discover how many parents blame and judge themselves for not being able to manage their anger. They think there is something wrong with them, compare themselves to others, and feel like their kids have lucked out.

You can share one important truth with them: anger management is a skill. Some of us pick vital skills up quicker than others, but all of us can learn to stay a step ahead of tense situations by knowing our own and others' triggers and employing specific tactics at every step of an anger-inducing situation.

You can help other parents control, regulate, and apply their emotions in useful ways. In doing so, you will enable them to parent calm, well-reasoned children who learn patterns of assertive, kind communication.

Many celebrities have shared stories with their fans of their highs and lows as parents. Hillary Duff, Jessica Alba, and Isla Fisher have all experienced tense moments while out and about with their kids. Charlize Theron was actually labeled a "Monster Mom" after she struggled to lead her crying child into her car while the paparazzi lights were flashing. Many have admitted that parenting can be tough and that it is definitely a learning process.

You may not have access to the media outlets that these stars have, but you do have a chance to let other parents know they are not abnormal, irrational, or bad parents. They simply need to learn or hone anger management skills that will serve them, not only with their kids, but also in their dealings with colleagues and adult family members.

Help readers understand that anger is an emotion that should be taken seriously.

By encouraging other readers to reign in their anger, understand where it is coming from, and how to best channel it, you can enable them to feel more confident and fulfilled as parents, spouses, and friends.

Thank you for your support. No parent is an island, and we can all help each other be a little kinder, more assertive, and loving with our children if we point them in the right direction.

Leave a review on Amazon.

4

CLEAR & EFFECTIVE COMMUNICATION IS IMPERATIVE

O ne of the most effective ways to bypass anger is to see things eye-to-eye with your children. You have to communicate effectively with them but also listen to what they have to say to you. When you are working as a team and you focus on solving problems instead of trying to "win" arguments, you can achieve far better results.

WHAT IS EFFECTIVE COMMUNICATION?

Effective communication involves more than just sharing information with someone else. It also requires us to understand the emotions that give rise to the words that we and others use (Robinson et al, 2020). Sometimes, we think that what we are saying is clear.

However, our intended message is one thing, and the message actually received by the other person can be something totally different. This can create conflict at work, in family relationships, and with friends and acquaintances.

Communication is not as mysterious as it seems, provided you learn the skills you need to build meaningful connections with others, prioritize trust and respect, learn to solve problems, and work on your mental health and well-being.

IDENTIFYING BARRIERS TO GOOD COMMUNICATION

The first step to communicating optimally with others is to identify common obstacles standing in your way. These can include:

▶ Unproductive body language

Many people don't value body language to the extent it merits. Research has shown that words, body language, and tone of voice account for 7%, 55%, and 38% of effective communication, respectively (Mehrabian, 1981). It is amazing to think that the gestures you use, the way you look at someone, or the positioning of your arms can turn someone off or make you seem angry or aggressive, when in fact your intentions are the complete opposite.

To be productive, body language needs to be consistent with your words and tone, as well as open and sincere. When a person is talking to you, look at them, avoid crossing your arms against your chest, and use tactics such as nodding once in a while and saying "Yes, I understand you," to show that you are fully present and interested in what they have today.

► **Displaying a Lack of Presence**

In his best-selling book, The Power of Now: A Guide to *Spiritual Enlightenment*, Eckhart Tolle wrote that "Stress is caused by being 'here' but wanting to be 'there' or being in the present but wanting to be in the future." If your child is trying to tell you something important and you are nodding but texting someone on your phone, answering an email, or watching a YouTube video, then it is easy to see how they can feel frustrated and unloved at a time in which they need your attention.

► **Listening in Order toTalk**

When you are discussing an important or tense topic with your children or spouse, you may have plenty to say and in fact, you may have thought out all your main points even before you started the discussion. Thus, when your loved ones speak, you may nod quickly, waiting for them to finish talking so you can deliver your well-planned speech. This amounts to talking (not communicating) since it flows in one direction. When you behave this way, people can tell that you aren't actually listening to them. Effective communication is a generous act—it is one of give-and-take. When someone is pouring their heart out, giving you feedback, or complaining about something, exercise empathy and show them that what they are saying is important to you.

THE PILLARS OF EFFECTIVE COMMUNICATION

Being a good communicator involves observing as much as it does using the right words, tone, and body language. There are four main tools you need to hone the art of effective communication (Robinson et al, 2020): working on stress relief, learning to identify and interpret body language, giving your full attention to others, and communicating assertively. When you are speaking to others, employ the following tools to ensure you communicate with them in a way they understand and are receptive to.

▶ **Learn to relieve your stress.**

You may be "bursting at the seams" to broach a topic with a loved one or colleague but you need to be clued in as to whether or not it's the right time. The fact that you can hardly contain what you need to say could be a sign you are stressed and need to pause to collect your thoughts and think of how you would like to phrase something.

Of course, sometimes, the choice isn't yours—you may need to "perform" well and demonstrate communication skills at a job interview, work situation, or impromptu situation that arises at home.

In order to stay calm under pressure, rely on techniques that can be lifesavers during tense moments. These can include practicing a few minutes of deep breathing, reminding yourself to pause instead of rushing through your thoughts and trying to get them all out at once, and asking the speaker to repeat what they have said if you need a little more time to process it.

Some people keep a stress ball to squeeze during times of tension while others find comfort in practicing progressive muscle relaxation. The latter involves squeezing or tightening muscles along the body (from your feet to your head) for a few seconds, then relaxing them.

Doing so can really show how much built-up tension you have been keeping inside. It can also help if you stop seeing a discussion or conflict as a "battle" but rather, a way for you and the other person to come to a consensus through compromise. Remember to speak clearly and concisely.

▶ Learn to watch out for and interpret body language.

How many times have you made an innocent comment to a friend, your spouse, or your children, only to have them snap back at you, seemingly out of nowhere? They could have been giving you a plethora of clues all the while, but you may have failed to notice them because these signals were nonverbal. If they cannot keep eye contact with you, they "close their body off" to you by crossing their arms or they turn their body (feet, torso, legs) away from you, they could be angry, disappointed, or frustrated.

You should also try to pay attention to your own body language. Use open, receptive body language when dealing with your child. This involves opening your eyes wide, turning your face and torso toward the speaker, keeping hands open and palms open and upturned, and pointing feet toward them (Morgan, 2011). You can also use tools such as touch (gently patting your child's back or putting your hand lightly on their shoulder while they are expressing sadness or otherwise talking about their emotions), speaking in a gentle tone of voice, and slightly arching your eyebrows to show you have a genuine interest in what they are saying.

▶ Give your full attention to others.

Knowing how to listen is the cornerstone of good communication, especially in a busy world in which it can sometimes seem that nobody has the time to listen to others. When talking with your kids, try to sit with your right ear facing them, since the right side of your body is connected to the left side of the brain (which plays a key role in emotion, language, and speech processing). Avoid interrupting, judging, criticizing, or blaming them, even if you don't completely agree with everything they are saying. Be open to feedback—it is an invaluable gift that people are often too afraid to give each other for fear of rejection.

▶ Communicate assertively.

It is important to listen but also to speak your mind since you should value your needs and concerns as much as those of others. It is okay to assert your limits, say no to something you feel is not good for your child, and express the things you don't like—so long as you maintain respect, kindness, and non-confrontational body language while doing so.

Two important assertiveness techniques are empathetic assertion (letting the person know you understand them but also letting them know your needs—if your child wants to stay up late you might say, "I understand you want to be with us for longer but you have to go to bed on time so you can feel energetic tomorrow.") and escalating assertion (being a bit firmer if you have to— for instance, you may gently tell your child, "I really want to give you time to play on your computer for half an hour but we already agreed that you would finish your homework before playing").

HOW TO COMMUNICATE EFFECTIVELY WITH OTHERS

Regardless of the setting you are in or the people you are speaking to (adults or children), effective communication comprises five key skills (Touro University Worldwide, n.d.). These are as follows:

* **Knowing how to listen**

Don't listen with your ears alone; be fully present when someone else is speaking, leaving aside worries and thoughts such as work tasks you have to do, the argument you had with your boss, or the household chores you need to complete.

- **Exercising empathy**

Try to put yourself in the speaker's shoes, eliminating judgment even if they feel or think differently about a situation. Imagine what it must feel like to be that person, with all their joys, fears, and myriad of complex emotions.

- **Encouraging others**

Praise others and encourage them to share ideas, make suggestions, and give feedback. Good communication is about more than what occurs when you are speaking. It starts way before that—in your daily dealings with others, the way you uplift them, and the way you strive to make them feel valued and respected.

- **Being aware of how others are feeling**

In order to know how a person is feeling, you need to know a bit about their lives. Even in a work setting, it pays to invest quality time in others so they can feel comfortable sharing their feelings with you when they are down and turn to you to share their good news as well.

Expressing an interest in others creates rapport and being discreet with the information they share with you helps to build trust.

- **Maintaining friendly body language**

Maintain eye contact the majority of the time that you are speaking with others and don't be afraid to use a little gesticulation to drive a point home. Stand straight and greet people with a smile, using touch appropriately when required (for instance, when someone is upset and may need calming down).

HOW TO COMMUNICATE EFFECTIVELY WITH YOUR CHILD

Children can be highly sensitive to your tone of voice, body language, and words. Choose words wisely. They can be hurtful or uplifting and they can be the difference between a fearful and a resilient child. Remember to use the following skills to make your child feel heard, understood, and loved:

- **Listen with your whole body.**

Show your child you care by sitting down next to them, holding their hand or giving them a gentle back rub if they are crying, and listening to their words and the emotions they reveal.

- **Pick up on the emotion.**

Pay attention to them and engage with their feelings. Try to understand the nature of what they cannot comprehend and help them identify feelings —this is a key element of emotional regulation. If they are crying and they say something like, "I hate Lily. She took my favorite toy car and broke it," you can say, "Oh, I see, you must be feeling angry. I would feel angry too. I know how much you love that toy."

- **Acknowledge your child's feelings.**

Children can have many emotions. They can feel delighted, sad, confident, furious, ashamed, scared, and more. Accepting these emotions is important (*Child & Adolescent Behavioral Health*, n.d.) because children should not feel like they have to be happy all the time. Talk about feelings regularly at home, asking your child to join you in identifying and labeling the emotions of their favorite characters from books, cartoons, or films. Finally, share your own emotions frequently, so that they learn that expression is a good thing, even in the case of negative emotions.

- **Teach them how to express feelings appropriately.**

Parents can have an instinct to rush in and "fix" things for their children or to try to end crying quickly. However, to a child in distress, nothing is quite as soothing as a parent who helps them identify their feelings and rewards positive emotional expression. Praise your child, saying something like, "Wow, you really handled your disappointment well. I saw that you were sad when Jamie's mom said she couldn't play today but you gave her a hug and said you could play tomorrow instead."

- **Delay correction and gather more information.**

If you jump the gun and start "fixing" a problem without listening to your child, they can feel even more frustrated. A good detective doesn't rush things. They observe and gather useful information until they see the light at the end of the tunnel.

- **Give your child space and time for self- regulation.**

If your child is expressing their feelings in an inappropriate manner, first acknowledge their feelings then briefly but decisively state the logical consequence of their actions. For instance, you might say, "I can see that you are furious because your brother tore your favorite book. That means that he will have to use a bit of his weekly pocket money to buy you a new one but it also means you will have to say sorry for hitting his hand when he gave the book back to you. Have a little quiet time and we can all talk about it when you're feeling calmer." Don't repeat your words or harp on. Make it short but sweet.

- **Look on the bright side of life.**

Even when it seems like Murphy's Law has struck, we can model positive behaviors, teaching our children to find the positives from every difficult situation. For instance, if your child has fought with a friend, ask them questions like "What can you learn from this?," "What can you do differently next time?," and "What is the solution to this problem?"

- **Teach your child relaxation techniques.**

Teach your child to battle stress through mindfulness meditation, kids' yoga, dance, and the visual arts. Give them the tools they need to explore these methods. There is an array of great apps, e-reader books, and CDs/audio files that can make mindfulness meditation fun and imaginative. Try out apps like *Headspace for Kids*; *Stop, Breathe & Think*; and *Mindfulness for Children*. They contain numerous activities of short and long duration with specific aims— including stress relief.

- **Teach your child to problem-solve.**

You can be Sherlock Holmes and your child Watson, or vice-versa when it comes to problem-solving. Show them how much fun this process can be and ask them to observe how good problem solvers often obtain the rewards or results they yearn for. Teach them the five crucial steps to follow:

- 1. Identify the problem clearly—for instance, "Lara takes my toys all the time but does not share hers."

- 2. Brainstorm solutions together: "What if we make an exchange program in which she can play with one of your toys if she lets you play with one of hers?"

- 3. Consider the ups and downs of each of the solutions you propose.
- 4. Start putting your plan into action.
- 5. Talk about it later and analyze the extent to which the solution worked or not.

When you are problem-solving, don't provide the solution; let your child take charge so they feel more empowered. When you have problems and they are appropriate to be shared with your child, ask your child for advice so they start feeling like capable problem solvers.

- **Adapt your problem-solving sessions to your child's age.**

Depending on your child's age you should have different goals when it comes to problem-solving. For instance, if you have children aged three to five, when they are upset, help them name and process their emotions and try a little collaborative problem-solving using creative play, stories, and the like. Children aged five to seven can start asking themselves more questions, including "What emotion am I feeling?," "What is the problem?," "What solutions are available?," What would occur if I...?," and "Which solution should I choose?" Children aged seven to nine can go a little further—for instance, by breaking down big problems into smaller ones. Older children can take part in creative problem-solving sessions, play chess, and learn coding. They might also enjoy taking part in group problem-solving tasks and games.

- **Avoid shaming your child.**

The social media boom has provided countless instances of parents shaming their children for "bad behavior." Never shame your child (privately or publicly) because this can have a long-term impact on your relationship and their self-esteem.

Keep trust strong by never telling others embarrassing stories about your child, sharing private conversations, or intentionally making a child feel useless or otherwise flawed. If you have unwittingly shared their private information, apologize, commit to not doing it again, and back your words up with actions. Examples of shaming statements include: "You're just as bad as your father!," "I'm so tired of you!," and "How dumb would you have to be to do what you did?" It is easy to see how painful these words can be.

- **Set aside judgment.**

Communicating effectively with others does not mean that you have to share their core beliefs and values. However, you do need to set aside any urge that may arise to blame or judge them. Even a challenging situation can result in a positive outcome and a sense of connection between two people who may have vastly different beliefs.

- **Build a positive mindset.**

Being optimistic is a quality that will help your child weather many of life's toughest challenges. Try to encourage optimism by interpreting daily experiences in a positive way. Children can feel happier about their own lives if they learn to set realistic goals and spend time doing things they enjoy and are good at. Make sure to give them the opportunity to join one or more extra-curricular clubs and activities if they express an interest in doing so.

You should also encourage them to try new things out so they build a sense of curiosity. Model this type of behavior by saying "yes" to new experiences and by showing your interest whenever they are excited about a new subject or activity.

Finally, model gratefulness. This will enable children to feel content with what they have and it will also encourage them to be more tolerant with people and situations. Ask children to tell you the highlight of their day and be just as interested in the experiences that made them sad or angry. Hone their empathy by trying to help them understand other people's views.

- **Help your child find support.**

Your children should know that they can always count on you when they are feeling down or when they need to talk about something that happened at school or playtime. However, they should be able to count on others as well. Let them know who they can turn to at school (for instance, a teacher or counselor), and in their private lives. They may be close to a grandparent or auntie and they should feel free to contact and approach family members if they feel like talking with someone with a new perspective.

- **Teach your child to learn positive lessons from negative circumstances.**

While encouraging children to be positive about life can help them be happier and healthier adults, teaching them to embrace negative experiences is helpful because challenges provide a vital opportunity

ANGER MANAGEMENT FOR PARENTS | 103

to learn lessons and pick up skills. If you notice that your child is upset, ask them what is wrong. Help them label feelings and work together to find solutions to the problem. Sometimes, all your children really want is someone who will listen to them.

- **Teach your child to be resilient.**

Show your children how to cope with problems calmly by setting a good example when you are tense. Let them express their anxious emotions and give them small strategies to try out when they need a little soothing. Praise them for facing their fears and experimenting with new strategies. Simply saying "I believe in you" will calm their fears and help them feel more able to solve their problems and withstand life's daily stressors.

TIPS FOR COMMUNICATING WHEN YOU ARE ALREADY IN THE HEAT OF THE MOMENT

Sometimes, conflicts can escalate rapidly and you and your child can find yourselves in the midst of a heated moment. If so, keep the following considerations in mind to lower stress and tension and to get back to a stage where you can employ problem-solving and additional solutions-based techniques:

- **Talk calmly and listen.**

    Speak clearly and check to see if your child under-
stands you. Remember to pause and listen openly to
what they have to say, too.

- **Be logical.**

    Children (particularly little children) aren't actually
setting out to make you lose your cool. They are not
"out to get you." Keep this in mind even when it seems
like your child is deliberately trying to provoke you.

- **Don't make generalizations.**

    Avoid sentences that use the words "You always..."
or "You never..." since it can make your child defensive.
Moreover, it fails to separate their actions from identity
and is a type of labeling.

- **Know the signs of an impending storm.**

    Recognize the sensations you feel when you are
angry. Common signs include a racing heart rate,
rapid breathing, teeth clenching, and more. During
this time, take rapid action. Count to 10 before
talking, breathing while you are doing so. Figure out
why you are so upset then try to calm down,
remembering that you are both here to solve a
problem.

If you are still about to explode, leave the room until you are calm. Let your child know you need a little break but that you will be back to talk things over when you can give them your best.

- **Use "I" instead of "you" language.**

It is easy to see how using the word "you" can make a statement sound like an accusation. For instance, there is a clear difference between saying "You drive me crazy when you leave your toys lying on the ground," and saying, "I feel that I am not appreciated when I see toys lying on the ground and I am expected to pick them up." The first statement seems like an attack while the second is a request for empathy.

- **Don't get defensive.**

Your child may criticize you, tell you they dislike you, and otherwise use hurtful words. When they do, it is usually because they are hurting and they want you to understand their pain. Focus on helping them learn the basics of emotional regulation. Try to find out what is really bothering them, asking questions calmly until you get to the crux of the matter.

- **Use humor to defuse heated situations.**

Have you ever been in the midst of a heated argument when someone says something or makes a funny noise and the two of you look at each other and burst out laughing? Humor is a powerful way of eliminating tension in an instant. Once you are having a giggle, try activities like play wrestling or a pillow fight. Don't use humor to tease or make jokes at your child's expense. Laughter is meant to unite, not divide.

- **Choose the right time and place.**

Don't confront your child with a problem when you're already stressed or tired from a long day at work. Give yourself at least 10 to 15 minutes to relax when you get home. Calm down and do something you enjoy then try tackling the problem.

SETTING CLEAR BOUNDARIES

It is much easier to maintain a respectful tone at home when boundaries and your individual roles within the situation (and conversation) are clear. Children are curious creatures who are still learning about their own (and your) limits and they may try to test the waters.

To establish firm boundaries with your child, adopt the following strategies:

- **Be trustworthy.**

Think about the time you first learned to ride a bike as a child. You may recall your mom or dad holding the back of your bike gently while walking or running by your side, slowly letting go for increasingly longer periods of time as you began gaining confidence and picking up the pace. You knew then that they would never fall; that they would be a buffer between you and the road. Building trust happens this way always. It is incremental and requires various small "tests" until it is established. There are specific strategies you can use (Carrero, n.d.) to build your child's trust in you.

- **Honor your promises.**

If you promised your child you would throw them a birthday party on their big day, do so, even if you aren't into parties. If you told them you would reward them for doing chores with lunch at their favorite burger restaurant on Saturday, take them. If you said you would pick them up at a friend's place at a designated time, be there and be punctual. Honoring promises (large and small) are an important way of letting your child know you care about their emotions and you will not let them down.

- **Show the respect you wish to receive.**

If you want your children to trust you, respect them always. Praise their efforts and honor their desire for independence. Your child should never fear you will shame or label them; otherwise, they will develop a defensive stance when dealing with you.

- **Be honest with your children.**

Most people would agree that it is impossible to trust a liar. Don't let your children catch you resorting to untruths. So-called "harmless lies" are sometimes told to save face but in reality, they can always be replaced by the truth through assertive communication techniques.

- **Listen to your child.**

We have provided examples of techniques to utilize when your child is trying to communicate with you. Once again, it is very hard for any human being to trust another who does not value them enough to listen to their important feelings and thoughts.

- **Be consistent.**

It doesn't pay to be kind and loving one day if you're going to explode and scream at your child the next day. Stability and consistency are the hallmarks of trustworthy individuals. People know where they stand with them. They are not afraid that the person will suddenly attack them, punish them, or demean them verbally, for no apparent reason. Nobody is perfect and you may have an off-day but when your child trusts you, they will know that the parent they know and love will be back to being their best self very soon—this will happen because they already trust you.

- **Break down big goals into smaller ones.**

Your parents didn't just throw you into the pool and tell you to swim. They fitted you with a life jacket and/or floaties, taught you how to kick your legs and blow bubbles under the water, then encouraged you to swim short (then increasingly longer) distances as they waited for you on the other side of the pool with their arms open. If you set children goals that are too big, they can feel overwhelmed and consider it unfair or feel inadequate. By giving them a series of small, achievable targets and being their safety net, they learn the value of reaching for the starts while knowing you will never let them fall.

• **Remember that less is more.**

There is a saying that goes, "Five rules respected 100% of the time are better than 20 rules with haphazard compliance." When it comes to children, apply this saying with extra care, since a child can find it much harder to focus than an adult. To measure a child's attention span, multiply their age by two or three. For instance, a six-year-old child may feel comfortable focusing for around 12 minutes *(British Council, n.d.)*. You should keep discussions short and sweet and keep goals simple and clear so that your child doesn't feel so overwhelmed or bored that they "tune out."

• **Be precise.**

Your child needs clear direction *(Peterson, n.d.)*. When you are confused, it flusters and frustrates them. To communicate clearly, know what you want to say, be willing to listen and do so actively (listening with your heart, not just your ears), and be aware of your own past experiences. How many times did you tell yourself you would never do something a parent did to you (for instance, shout, shame, or raise your voice?). Keep these stories in mind and try not to repeat past mistakes.

- **Involve children in boundary setting.**

When children are young, boundary setting is simple because it usually involves a small and basic set of rules —for instance, you may instruct a toddler not to hit, bite, or invade others' body space. As they get older, however, boundaries can become more complex and understanding others' rights, needs, and wants, involves higher skills such as empathy. The latter is a quality that can be learned and the best "classroom" for it is real life.

If you are at a playground and your child pulls a toy out of another child's hands, the child may begin to cry. This is the perfect moment to step in and ask your child, "How do you think Mary feels when you pull her toy away? Do you think it might be better to ask her to share next time instead of pulling the toy out of her hands?" You can also take advantage of the situation to teach your child the essentials of empathy. For instance, you might ask, "Would you like it if Mary pulled your pail and shovel out of your hand?" When you ask these questions, don't do so with an angry or annoyed tone of voice. Your child should see them as authentic questions and hopefully give answers and a pledge to not repeat the action. Under your gentle prompting, they can learn to apologize to the child whose toy they took.

During quiet moments, you can take the opportunity to talk about a few boundaries that all people have. For instance, it is not okay to touch others if they don't want to be touched, rough and tumble games (like pillow fights) are only okay if two people want to play them, and nobody likes to be interrupted when they are talking.

Encourage your children to set and express their own boundaries. If they don't like being hugged by other children, ask them, "How do you think you can let Sam know that you don't like being hugged?" When your child lets you know their limits, respect them. Don't force them to kiss or hug family friends if they feel uncomfortable doing so.

Ensure that your children have friends from diverse backgrounds. Doing so will teach them that limits and boundaries can vary from culture to culture and that even if these limits are different to one's own, they should be respected. Having friends who are different from oneself can also help one "relax" and learn to value the essential things in life such as trust, friendship, and laughter.

Because you are a mirror children see themselves in, set a good example by respecting boundaries and defending your own on a daily basis. For instance, if someone at the supermarket tries to cut in on you, you can say, "Sorry but I was next in line. I have been standing behind this gentleman for a few minutes." Your child will notice how you respect others (even in an undesirable situation while still standing up for your own rights politely) and they will take the same care with others in social situations.

- **Draw up a contract.**

    All contracts have benefits for all the parties who sign it and so, too, should your contract with your child. A contract is beneficial because it clearly lays out expectations and rewards and can be turned to in the event of confusion. Under its terms, your child may have to fulfil certain obligations (including those related to schoolwork, safety, following directions, responsibilities and chores, and managing emotions). If your child fulfils these obligations, they can obtain points that will entitle them to a reward you both agree upon.

    When drafting the contract, stay in control so that rewards are reasonable. There shouldn't be so many clauses that the contract becomes confusing. Choose the areas you most wish to focus on and be fair with the number of tasks children are required to complete. The duties you list should be age-appropriate.

For instance, an eight-year-old may be asked to complete basic chores (such as tidying up, helping parents make meals on the weekends, and making their bed) while a 13- year-old may be asked to limit the amount of time they spend on electronics, complete homework assignments on time, and feed the dog.

- **Post the rules.**

Remember to post the contract in a spot that you and your children can easily access. This way, you can consult it if in doubt, so as to eliminate confusion.

- **Recognize appropriate behavior.**

Praise your child frequently every time they fulfil a duty or behave in a way that is stipulated in your contract. Remind them that they are doing well and are well on the way to achieving their goals.

- **Avoid labeling children as "good" and "bad."**

In Chapter Two, we highlighted the effect that labeling can have on parents and children. Labeling your child as "bad" when they do or say something ties their identity to one fleeting moment.

One bad day does not define your children. Labeling a child as "good," meanwhile, can put plenty of pressure on them to keep conforming to your high standards. Doing so can also lead a child to suppress their feelings, which can harm their character development in the long run.

- **Don't compare your children to others.**

One of the most painful things you can do to your child is compare them to their classmates and friends, since this can severely impact their self-worth and make them feel second-best. Let them know that there are many different types of intelligence, abilities, and talents and that everyone is a star that shines in the universe. If they are talented at the piano, they are great writers, or they draw beautifully, give them the tools they need to pursue their talents or hobbies but never tie their self-worth to grades, abilities, or talents. Doing so can actually take the joy out of something they love and make it a chore or even a source of rebellion against what they may perceive as your attempt to control them.

- **Never undermine the other parent.**

When you shout at your partner, call them names, or show them disdain, your kids take it all in like a sponge. Consider children to be natural "hypocrite hunters." You can't expect them to be empathetic, sensitive, and gentle when you don't extend these behaviors to your own spouse.

Your behavior could also amount to parental alienation, which occurs when one parent badmouths the other parent; limits the amount of time they spend with children; or implies that the other parent is bad, fearful, or dishonest.

Parents who alienate others often use the "good cop, bad cop" tactic to get closer to their children at the expense of the co-parent. We have mentioned many strategies you can use to regulate your emotions and help your children manage theirs but these will be less effective if you undermine the other parent and negate their role in your child's life.

An example of very subtle (but still harmful) parental alienation is as follows: your spouse, Henry, is working from home and has a desk area in the living room, where all your children are playing. Henry has a big report to finish so he asks the kids to play more quietly. You say, "Come on Henry, they're children. It's normal for them to make noise."

When Harry repeats that he cannot work with the racket going on, you say, with a sigh, "Oh well, kids, let's go to the garden and play on the swings. We can have fun again later when Daddy finishes working." Clearly, this statement puts the blame on Henry and makes him seem like a party pooper when what he is asking for is not only reasonable but also a necessary work obligation.

A child who is used to taking sides and forming part of triangles will find it more difficult to have successful relationships. They may create "bad guys" where they don't exist or try to get closer to one person by forming an "alliance" against someone else. To help your children be healthy, happy, balanced adults, teach them the power of unity and shun divisiveness and toxic triangulation.

To ensure you and your spouse are on the same page, have meetings and talk about your children, sharing concerns, successful strategies, and funny stories. Children are a never-ending source of joy so if you have any special moments with them, make sure to fill your partner in afterward. The stronger your child's bond is with both of you, the more likely they are to feel that they will always be safe on that bike, because one or both of you will always be there to catch them when they fall.

5

YOUR CHILD WILL MIRROR YOUR ENERGY

It may be hard to believe that anyone could admire you so much but it is true—you are your " child's everything." A 2018 survey *(Explore Learning, 2018)* asked children who their biggest hero was and 39% of girls answered that it was their mom, followed by their dad (17%). Around 30% of boys, meanwhile, saw Dad as their most admired being, with moms coming in a close second at 29%. Because children idolize your every move, they act how you act and they continue to do so for as long as you allow them to.

YOUR CHILD IS YOUR PERFECT MIRROR

Children are always watching and observing their parents *(Akers, 2020)*. They are learning everything from you: how to assert their needs, express their emotions, spend their free time, socialize with others, and interact with the natural world around them. When they say something that makes your whole body shake with laughter, they are mirroring your sense of humor. When they display a natural curiosity about animals, plants, and flowers, it is because they are inspired by your curiosity and love of nature. When they pet a friend's dog or cat with gentleness, it is probably because they have seen you exercise the same love, care, and respect when petting animals.

You cannot take the credit for the good and shun the things you don't like about your child. All they are doing is holding up a mirror to you—and you may not necessarily like everything you see. When they display "bad" behaviors like raising their voice, slamming the door behind them, or letting a little insult or derogatory word slip from their tongue ("You ruined the puzzle, dummy!") that also comes from you. Don't be too hard on yourself, though, for you are also holding a mirror in your hand—in it, your own parents are reflected.

One of the most enlightening days of your life as a parent may be the day you tell your child not to do something and they answer you with the words, "Well, that's what you do."

How can you honestly ask a child to stop telling their sibling to "Shut up" if, just a few hours previously, you told both your kids to do just that when they were getting a bit too rowdy and noisy for your taste?

CHILDREN'S BRAINS ARE STILL DEVELOPING

The fact that kids are a mirror is both a challenge and a gift. It is a challenge because it prompts us to truly see the impact our behavior has on others and a gift because children are malleable. There is time to change —a child's brain is not fully developed until they are 23. Therefore, if your seven-year-old or pre-teen seems like a real firecracker that "can't be tamed," start working on yourself. Doing so will enable you to be a better guide for them in the future. Don't rush. There is so much time left for them to learn from you.

CHILDREN PICK UP ON YOUR STRESS

Children may still be in the process of development, yet they are also very aware. For instance, they know when you're suppressing emotions. When you think you are "putting up a good act," you may actually be transmitting your stress to them. A study by Washington State University researchers *(Waters et al, 2020)* found that suppressed emotions were linked to less warmth and engagement between parents and children. If you feel anxious or worried, don't say "I'm fine," as this will only make you less available to your child. The researchers stated that children find it more comforting when parents validate their feelings instead of immediately rushing in to solve their problems. Parents, they advised, should allow children to regulate their own emotions while also permitting themselves to be frustrated and emotional sometimes.

CHILDREN NEED BOUNDARIES

Some parents find the pre-teen and early teen years particularly challenging because children can test limits during this time. As they reach out for independence, kids may experiment with hairdos, fashions, musical tastes, and other means of expression. Enjoy these moments, since your child's choices reveal a part of them that is all their own—one that may be influenced by sources apart from yourself. Despite conceding that your children are in the process of defining and developing their identities, however, know that they still need (and expect) you to set boundaries.

BOUNDARIES AND PARENTING STYLES

A research group led by academics from Japan conducted a survey *(Kobe University, 2016)* to discover the extent to which parenting styles affect the happi-ness of children. The scientists divided parenting into six categories:

- Supportive—a style of parenting that gives children lots of positive attention, as well as high levels of trust, and quality time.

- Strict—this parenting style demonstrates medium-to-high interest in children but involves low levels of independence. Trust levels stand at medium-to-high, and the child is given many rules to follow.

- Indulgent—these parents are lenient, spend an average amount of time or longer with their children, and trust their children implicitly.

- Easygoing—this style is also lenient but involves low levels of interest in children and little time spent together.

- Harsh—a style involving strictness, low levels of trust in a child, and giving a child little independence.

- Average—a style that averages out key factors.

The researchers found that children of "supportive" parents were more likely to enjoy academic success, have higher-paying jobs, and be happy. Children of "strict" parents also enjoyed material and academic success but were unhappier and showed higher levels of stress. The study is testimony to the importance of being supportive and loving. Rules are an important part of communication but children should have a good balance between expectations and independence. When setting boundaries, remind your children that you are a team and that everyone needs to do their share to achieve common and individual goals.

The idea that fair rules are positive is backed by other studies, one of which *(Slone & Shoshani, 2017)* found that even children who had been through extremely traumatic events benefited from warm and authoritative (as opposed to authoritarian) parenting styles. Consider discipline and emotional support to be the "yin and yang" of good parenting.

CHILDREN CAN MIRROR YOUR FEAR

Your child may be acting up on a given day because they fear something. They may be unfazed by typical things like "the monster who sleeps under their bed," yet deeply scared of being left alone, making friends at school, anxiety, academic and sporting expectations, and so much more.

These fears will be exacerbated if they see you as an insecure, fearful person who lacks anger management and conflict resolution skills. Studies have shown *(Muris et al, 1996)*, for instance, that parental fear plays an important role in modeling children's fear.

Ensure that your children feel safe and secure in their environment so they can learn, play, and grow in a healthy way. Early exposure to circumstances that cause fear and chronic anxiety can disrupt the correct development of a child's brain, affecting their ability to learn, problem-solve, and interact with others. Fear affects the brain architecture of learning and memory. The prefrontal cortex, which regulates thoughts, emotions, and actions, is particularly vulnerable to brain chemicals produced by stress.

Fear also affects the amygdala (which triggers emotional responses) and the hippocampus (which controls short-term memory). High levels of cortisol (a stress hormone) affect growth and performance and, when present at chronically high levels, is linked to a host of conditions—including type 2 diabetes, obesity, and inflammation.

Open communication, trust, and quality time must all be present if your child is to express their fears and overcome them. For instance, if your child is moving to a new school and they are scared of making friends, why not get to know other parents in your area so you can organize play dates and give your child a better chance of fitting in once school starts?

MODELING POSITIVE BEHAVIORS

If you want your child to be a good learner, ask yourself when the last time was that you picked up a book, became authentically curious about a subject, or took a course. If you expect your child to read but you spend most of your time surfing the web, they may not develop an interest in the literary arts.

Demonstrate your fundamental values and beliefs through your behavior. For instance, if you have a daughter and you want her to be aware of the importance of women's rights and equality, make sure that things are fair in the home—especially if you have a son. Everyone—regardless of gender—should have chores and responsibilities at home. If you have boys, teach them how to cook and clean. Not only will their sisters feel like they are part of a fair team, but the future partners of your sons will also feel like their rights, wants, and needs are being duly respected.

Other positive traits children can benefit from learning include being true to one's identity, treating oneself with self-respect, and being self-confident.

Self-respect is a wide concept and can include everything from feeding your body healthy foods right through to exercising regularly, giving yourself a break once in a while, and having hobbies that excite and motivate you intellectually. Self-confidence, meanwhile, can be demonstrated by standing up for what you believe in while speaking respectfully to others. This doesn't mean getting into arguments with people at the shops, on the road, or in the street. It simply means making decisions in line with what you think and believe and saying "no" when you believe a request crosses your boundaries or makes you feel like you are doing something you don't want to.

When you interact with your children, ask yourself what kind of adult you want them to become. That adult is who you need to be. "Do as I say, not as I do" simply won't work. Moreover, it can be difficult to respect someone who places high demands on you but who isn't willing to "walk the talk" themselves. An analogy you may find useful is that of bosses and their employees. Bosses who are authoritarian, those who micromanage, and those who expect employees to work "above and beyond" expectations while evading hard work themselves are often disliked. Moreover, they don't motivate staff to do their best, since they tend to reap all the praises and rewards, undervaluing their team.

A great boss, on the other hand, is supportive, trusting, grateful, and complimentary toward workers. Above all, they lead by example and are the kind of professional that their employees aspire to be. Try to be this type of leader for your child. Their happiness and well-being depend on it.

TEACHING CHILDREN GRATEFULNESS

"Gratitude is riches, complaint is poverty," said iconic Hollywood actress, Doris Day, and science has since backed this claim over and over. Studies have shown *(George Mason University, 2009)* that the key to happiness is gratitude—a quality that can be defined as thankfulness and joy. In the study, lead author, Todd Kashan, defined the three elements that were essential for creating happiness and meaning in life. They are: "meaningful relationships, gratitude, and living in the present moment with an attitude of openness and curiosity." If, indeed, these are the secrets of a happy life, what greater gift could you give your child than managing your emotions so that the next time your child holds that mirror up to your face, you like what you see?

One study (American Psychological Association, 2012) found that grateful teens enjoy numerous mental health benefits. Scientists asked 700 students aged 10 to 14 to complete questionnaires at the commencement of the study and four years later to compare data. When comparing the results of the least grateful and most grateful children, they found that grateful kids showed a 15% heightened sense of meaning in their lives, were 15% more pleased with their life overall, and 17% happier and more hopeful about their lives. They also had a 13% drop in negative emotions and a 15% drop in symptoms of depression. Even children who didn't start the study with a thankful attitude were capable of developing gratitude over time. Those who learned the art of gratefulness showed important mental health benefits—including reductions in behaviors such as missing school, getting detentions, and abusing alcohol and substances.

REPLACING ANGER WITH A HEALTHIER EMOTIONAL STATE

If repressing anger doesn't help, how can you deal with negative emotions positively? In earlier chapters, we highlighted how triggers can result in angry outbursts and we delved into the importance of defining your own triggers. Negative emotions are more than the result of a trigger. They also result from the way we interpret a situation. The key to emotional regulation is to see the role we have played in becoming so angry.

Is there any way we either avoid unnecessary triggers or reframe situations that regularly cause us stress?

To replace anger, try to change what you can. If you have a stressful job, for instance, hone your time management skills to perfection so you meet deadlines comfortably. Give yourself set times to complete your daily goals and use apps like Clockily, Rescue Time, or Remember the Milk to reduce time wastage and manage tasks.

Sometimes, stress is caused by failing to assert yourself or make your limits clear. Be true to yourself and say what you need at the right time, so that frustrations don't build up. Finally, make sure to have many healthy outlets for stress. We will suggest specific stress-busting activities in Chapter Seven though the important thing is to find your preferred methods of stress relief and to be generous with yourself so that you have enough time to pursue these activities.

KEEPING YOUR ANGER IN CHECK WHEN KIDS HAVE A MELTDOWN

When your child has a meltdown, try to lower tensions. As a role model, it is your job to change the tone and vibe of the moment to a more relaxed and reasoned one. You can do this by keeping your voice calm, soothing your child, and letting them know you understand what they are going through. When you feel like you're at your wit's end or you have had a day filled with tension and triggers, remember that your child's tantrum is not a personal attack. All children have tantrums and once these start, they can be incredibly difficult to quell. See an outburst as an opportunity to teach your child how to recognize, accept, analyze, and finally, control their feelings. This will get easier as children mature and develop key abilities such as self-awareness.

REDIRECTING YOUR CHILD'S ANGER

When a toddler is in the middle of a meltdown, try to redirect their attention. For instance, if your child is screaming because they broke a toy, tell them, "Raising your voice is never good. Why don't we go to the garden and water your vegetables?" Try the following steps when your child next has a tantrum:

- Before redirecting your child to a new thought or activity, take a moment to breathe deeply and calm your nerves. Doing so will help your child see that tantrums don't have power over you.

- Speak assertively, letting your child know you are serious while giving them time to quiet down.

- Reassure your child that it is okay to be upset, saying something like, "I, too, would be upset if my best friend couldn't come to play today."
- Try to reduce triggers. The sight of a broken toy, for instance, may keep your child "stuck" in a negative state. Direct your child to another part of the house, preferably outdoors, so the source of their trigger is not so immediate.
- Head to a new space that is full of new things that can fascinate your child. Nature is a particularly powerful stress buster so a walk outside can do the trick when your child is upset.
- Prevent tantrums by noticing triggers (which can include specific times of the day and situations). Try to work out the cause of repeated tantrums—for instance, your child may feel tired after lunch and may simply need a nap. If a particular game gets them frustrated, they may need time until they are mature enough to play it.
- Be patient and try out strategies more than one time. Practice makes perfect and nobody knows your child like you do. Little by little, you can perfect the art of preventing and dealing with tantrums in the way that works best for your child.

WHY YOU SHOULD STAY CALM

It can be very hard to stay calm and go against your instinct to match your child's anger or to try to shout over them. However, when you lose your cool, you engage in self-sabotage and impair your child's ability to manage their own anger. You react instead of act, teach your child that shouting is the expected reaction to stress, and reinforce negative core beliefs. If every time your child is tense, you lose your cool, your child can begin to think that they deserve this type of treatment. They can develop beliefs like, "My parents shout at me because I'm bad and don't deserve to be treated better."

Your child can also learn how to "wear you down" through tantrums and yelling. Remaining composed, on the other hand, equalizes conflicts and prioritizes teamwork. Staying calm promotes emotional closeness. To boost calmness, practice the emotional skills we discussed in Chapters Two and Three. When a tantrum is at its apex, pause. Be aware of your own body signals telling you that your anger is escalating, breathe. When you are a little calmer, act. Express your thoughts and wishes assertively while always putting empathy and a desire to connect at the forefront.

CALMNESS AS A QUALITY

Calmness is more than a reaction and more than an emotion. It can become a trait if you take the steps you need to in order to make it become a part of your personality. Being authentically calm is a journey and it starts with greater self-awareness *(Pruess, n.d.)*. As you mature as a human being, you may find that many times, the issue that needs changing is not the circumstances and stressors you cannot avoid in your daily life, but rather, how you process them and react to them. If you blame your children, colleagues, social media, chores that need doing, and other matters for your displaced anger, it's a good sign you need to pause, analyze, reframe, and act assertively or move on.

Once you are more self-aware, you can apply the emotional regulation techniques we highlighted in previous chapters (these include recognizing your triggers and taking yourself to a safe place through a reappraisal of the situation). One useful piece of advice is to place a hand over your heart as you breathe deeply and repeat, "We are okay," before letting your agitation result in an outburst.

Embrace the array of small but powerful actions, tools, and strategies that you find useful. You might find that relaxing therapeutic-grade essential oils like lavender quell your stress. Going for a run may make you feel renewed. Having lunch with your group of friends and sharing stories and laughs may help you feel more grounded and complete as an individual. Go for experiences that motivate you as a complete human being who is a parent but also a friend, athlete, film lover, avid reader, botany enthusiast, and more. Sometimes, all it takes to make you feel "whole" again is a hug.

Finally, keep the ultimate goal in mind—to be the very best parent you can be. This will keep you grounded and committed. Don't let one bad day or setback interfere with your larger vision. Your kids are your legacy. Enable them to be the best persons they can be by giving them all the tools they need to be calm, confident, and happy.

6

CHILDREN JUST WANT TO BE LOVED

The most important thing children need is simple —for you to love them. Sometimes, parents can lose sight of this fact, spending valuable time and energy on trying to create the perfect "mini-version" of themselves. In the end, the little choices you make along the way do not matter as much as giving a child the ultimate gift—that of feeling loved, secure, and comfortable "in their own skin." In what ways does love benefit a child *(Oliver, 2016)* and why is it so important to show them how you feel about them?

LOVE BOOSTS HEALTHY BRAIN DEVELOPMENT IN CHILDREN

From the time your child is a baby, giving them love and creating strong bonds is vital—as found in a study by neuroscientists at the Washington University School of Medicine in St. Louis *(Luby et al, 2012)*. The researchers conducted brain scans on children, finding that those who had been nurtured by their mothers had a hippocampus that was 10% larger than those who had not. The hippocampus is an important part of the brain because it is the main structure involved in the activation of the autonomic nervous system (an involuntary nervous system that controls the release of stress hormones). The study was the first to reveal actual anatomical changes in the brain resulting from a lack of nurturing. The findings are a powerful reminder of the importance of "getting it right" from the start.

Another study undertaken at the University of Iowa *(Kochanska & Kim, 2012)* found that infants who have a close relationship with at least one parent are less likely to display problematic behaviors or have emotional problems when they are older. The findings showed that the children can be close to either parent to reap big emotional dividends. The researchers stated that the first two years of life are vital for parents to form loving, secure relationships with their child.

This period "appears to be critical to the child's social and emotional development," said researcher, Grazyna Kochanska.

A LOVING HOME BOOSTS *SELF-CONFIDENCE*

If you really want your children to feel good about themselves, bestowing lavish praise on them won't do the trick, love will. Researchers at the University of Amsterdam *(Brummelman & Thomaes, 2017)* found that too much praise can actually hamper self-esteem while treating children warmly can make them feel on top of the world.

From the time children are toddlers, they develop a sense of self. They see this "self" as unique and separate from the body, and stable throughout time. As they grow, their self-concept begins to become more pronounced and they can become more aware of how they differ from others. Some children like what they see in the mirror. They can see themselves as malleable (capable of growing and changing). Others see their abilities as fixed in time. The researchers in the study reported that although the precise origins of a child's self-concept are impossible to identify, one thing we do know is that part of this self-concept is based on their relationships with others. Parents who display warmth, are excited about their child's interests, and enjoy quality time with them, make children feel seen, heard, and valued.

When parents display their appreciation and love for their children by praising them frequently—for instance, by saying "Wow, you did so well in your exam!," "Way to go for winning the swim race!" and the like, a child can feel like their parents only love them when they "win" or achieve top results. This does not mean, of course, that parents should not praise their children. The key takeaway from the study is that warmth and quality time should be the main ways through which your love for your children is expressed, rather than achievement-based praise.

LOVE AND THE GROWTH MINDSET

Children should not feel that success in life is based on the abilities they are born with. Doing so can keep them stuck from growth and positive change. They should be encouraged to believe that goals can be achieved through commitment and hard work. They should also know that most skills—ranging from sports to reading or mathematics—can be improved. Doing so can help prevent children from putting themselves into self- limiting "boxes" such as the "athlete box" ("I'm great at football but I am a bad student") and similar illusory boxes. Start praising your child's efforts ("Wow! You studied so hard for your exam. Your commitment was impressive!") as opposed to praising results ("Yes! You got an 'A' on your exam! I was expecting no less.")

YOUR RESPONSE TO FAILURE MATTERS

If you want your child to achieve success when they are older, monitor your beliefs. New research from the journal *Psychological Science* (Haimovitz & Dweck, 2016) found that parents' beliefs about whether failure is a positive or negative thing guide their children's views about their own intelligence. Parents should endorse a growth mindset by having a positive, constructive reaction to their child's struggles. Lead researcher, Kyle Haimovitz, stressed that children are very much in tune with how their parents view failure. You cannot really instill a growth mindset in your child if you do not help them see failure as an opportunity for positive change.

A LACK OF PARENTAL WARMTH IS LINKED TO HEALTH RISKS

We know the positive things that love can achieve but what about the opposite—what happens when a child lacks parental warmth? Research by University of California Los Angeles Health Sciences researchers (Car- roll et al, 2013) showed that the effects of a lack of warmth from parents can last a lifetime. When a child experience "toxic stress," they have a higher risk of elevated cholesterol, cardiovascular disease, metabolic syndrome, and other conditions which can wrest from their quality of life and even shorten their lifespan.

On the other hand, love is so powerful that it can reduce the impact of abuse. Lead author, Judith E. Carroll explained that children who are loved by parents or guardians, may be more protected from the harms of abuse and have a smaller risk of developing abuse-related health problems than children who are not loved.

CHILDREN ALSO NEED POSITIVE ATTENTION

Love is a feeling but it needs to be manifested in a productive way and when it comes to children (and indeed all human beings) it should be expressed through positive attention—which involves responding to your loved one with warmth and interest (Raising Children Network, n.d.). Doing so will enable them to feel like they are loved, leading to optimal development and self-image. Positive attention doesn't have to be pencilled into your schedule. It is something you can practice every day with your child.

WAYS TO SHOW POSITIVE ATTENTION

Positive attention can be given both verbally and non-verbally. In Chapter Five, we mentioned the importance of body language when dealing with children. To make them feel valued, make eye contact and use caring facial expressions. Smile, hug your child, and show that you share their interests. Words of affirmation—letting your child know how much they mean to you—are also important. When your kids run up to show you a drawing they have completed, or they want to sing you a song, let your face light up with enthusiasm so they feel special.

POSITIVE ATTENTION DIFFERS DEPENDING ON YOUR CHILD'S AGE

Babies need a different type of attention than preteens or teens. Much of the positive attention they require involves soothing, play (repeating sounds, for instance), and the exploration of the things they love. For instance, if they love playing with the toy hanging above their crib, lie down beside them and join them in reaching for the toy, making sounds and speaking words that show that you find it fascinating too.

As babies turn into toddlers, they start talking and understanding the words you may use to boost their self-confidence.

When your child has finished a finger painting, show your enthusiasm with words like, "Wow! That is so pretty and colorful! I want to make one too!" You can also make suggestions without "correcting" what they have done. For instance, you might suggest using different types of crayons, paint, and other materials, without making a qualitative statement like "It will look better if you use this crayon." Because your child is starting to talk, you should start honing your listening skills, allowing them time to express what they want to say. As children reach preschool age, you can join them in a host of activities—ranging from building towers from blocks to painting plants and flowers. During this time, children can start to comprehend what emotions are. When you have finished playing, mention how you feel, saying something like, "Oh I'm so sad, I have to go to work now!" When you return, put your hands in the air and say, "Yay! I'm so happy I'm back and I can play with you. Give me a big hug!"

School-aged children and pre-teens have more complex needs—including letting you know how their day went at school, talking about friends, and expressing interests. This is a time in which sharing interests with your child (think bike riding, cooking, scrapbook making, reading, digital art creation, and more) can strengthen your bond.

Spending time together on common hobbies has the added benefit of providing a relaxed setting in which you can discover things you never knew about each other. When your child is taking part in these activities with others, make observations and comment positively on the way they interact socially. For instance, you might say, "I noticed that Emma really enjoyed it when you sang your favorite song for her. It's nice that you like to share your lovely voice with your friends," or "I saw you share your snack with Joe. That was so nice of you!"

As a whole, positive attention is all about connection and fun. When you are with your child, try to avoid judging or criticizing. You can say anything you want to, provided you do so in a positive manner instead of a critical one. The benefits of spending quality time together are cumulative. Because your child trusts you and knows you love them, when you do need to point out a behavior that may need correction, they are more likely to listen to you and to believe that you are really trying to help them instead of judging and shaming them. A strong bond will also help your child listen to you with an open heart when you teach them conflict resolution skills.

VALIDATION IS A POWERFUL PARENTING TOOL

Validation as a psychological tool was proposed in the book *Cognitive-Behavioral Treatment of Borderline Personality Disorder (Linehan, 1993)*. In this book, author Marsha Linehan, Ph.D., recommended that therapists make their clients feel validated by letting them know that their responses make sense, that the therapist accepts these responses, and that they are to be taken seriously. It is easy to see how this concept can work equally well when parents are dealing with children. When your child complains about something and you tell them you can imagine how they are feeling and that you understand why they feel the way they do, they feel valued and heard and they learn to understand that your love for them is unconditional.

Validating is accepting that your child can have an experience, day, or moment in life that they find challenging —without trying to "snap them out of it" or imply they are overreacting. For instance, if you have a teen who has just felt the disappointment of "breaking up" with their crush, if you say, "Everyone's been through that, just enjoy your time with friends and don't give it too much thought," your child can feel distant from you because you are clearly reducing the importance of something that matters deeply to them.

Instead, tell them you understand how painful a breakup is. Try to avoid giving advice until they ask for it and give them the time they need to "let it all out" and run ideas and strategies by you.

Validation does not mean agreeing with everything your child says or allowing them to get away with behavior that lies outside your household's rules. For instance, in the example above, your heartbroken child may ask if she can go to the movies with her friends. If she has an exam the next day and needs to get up early, validate the fact that she is feeling down but let her know that it is better to leave the movie outing for the weekend.

Validate your child even when they are angry and frustrated or expressing themselves too effusively. Doing so will bring the tension down. Sometimes, all your child needs is someone to understand them; someone who isn't rushing in to fix their problem or comprehend the sometimes complex, mysterious nature of relationships. By sitting with your child, holding them, and telling them you are sorry they are sad/angry/disappointed, you can create memories your child will cherish for years. Try to recall the tough times in your life when a parent or family member may have been there for you. During these moments, you may have felt a depth of love that you will recall with fondness for the rest of your life.

SHOWING YOUR CHILD LOVE

If you've read the best-selling book *The 5 Love Languages (Chapman, 2010)*, then you know that people have different preferred means of giving and receiving love. The book contains a useful list of primary "love languages" used by people. These are: words of affirmation (expressing affection through the spoken word), quality time (spending time with someone while giving them our undivided attention), physical touch (expressing love through hugs, holding hands, touching an arm, and the like), acts of service (doing favors for others like doing the dishes, taking them to ballet practice, or repainting a broken but cherished toy), and receiving gifts (many people find it incredibly touching when someone goes out of their way to get them something they want, need, or expressed an interest in some time ago). The book postulates that sometimes, conflicts, pain, and disappointment can arise when we have a primary love language that differs vastly from that of our loved ones.

Arguably the most important lesson in the book is that when you want to make someone happy, you have to do so in a way they understand. That means being flexible and sometimes using a love language that is not your first choice.

This is a good tip to keep in mind when trying to express affection for your child. Your love language may be "giving and receiving gifts" and you may be excited about giving your child a beautiful bracelet you recently purchased from a luxury store. However, ask yourself if they are as enthusiastic about jewelry as you are. They may actually be happier if you spend a day with them at the mall, watch a movie, and have lunch together. This is not to say that their love language is "better" or "more meaningful." It is simply different. Think about it this way: If your child has always wanted to learn to paddleboard, why get them a piano for their birthday instead of the experience of their dreams?

When working out how to show your child love, simply listen to them. Give them a "yes" day—an experimental day in which you agree to say "yes" to all reasonable requests. What did your child ask for? A set of headphones? A visit to the local dog shelter to walk and possibly foster a dog? Time together and plenty of hugs and loving words? Observe your child's behaviors when they feel loving toward you— their choices will provide key information as to how they enjoy giving and receiving love.

There is also a small list of tried-and-tested activities that almost all children love. These include:

- **Spending quality time together**

This can involve playing, creating a project, or going for a swim together. Quality time involves full presence and mindfulness. It is all about "being in the here and now" with no greater priority than enjoying "the spectacular now" with your child.

- **Giving your child importance**

Show them you are really interested in whatever activity you are carrying out together. Tell them things like, "I really like how you made the lookout in that Lego tower. It creates a sense of mystery and we can put our mini-figures into them," "Your idea to swirl the icing around in the cupcake was fantastic. Look at how cute they look when they are baked," or "Wow! I can see that you really dislike that crayon. How about trying this one? It is smooth and waxy." Let them know you are taking notice of the small decisions they are making and be sincere in your praise. Remember, children are very quick to spot inauthenticity.

- **Finding things to admire in your child**

Try to reframe the qualities society deems "undesirable," celebrating the uniqueness of your child's personality. For instance, people may say, "Oh your daughter Laura is so sweet but she's so naughty. She's always running around and just can't keep still." Don't let their words affect the positive light which you shine on your child. Tell your friend that you think it is fantastic that your child is so energetic. If your child has heard their critical remarks, say something like, "I love how energetic you are! I get tired just walking a mile but you can run that and still jump around."

As a rule, be very careful about letting "playground talk" let you down. It is a fact that others can be competitive and their own insecurity may prompt them to compare your child's behavior to that of their children. Avoid people who do not accept your child, who criticize and judge them, and above all, make you feel like a "bad parent" because your child does not conform to their standards. Exercise self-love and be confident in your positive beliefs. Nobody has the right to make you feel ashamed, uncomfortable or scared that your child will do something they do not approve of (for instance, "fidget in their chair" or "talk too loudly"). The last thing your child needs is someone influencing their parents against them. Of course, be open to feedback but make sure it comes from the heart.

- **Walking in your child's shoes**

It is very hard to be annoyed at a child if you walk a minute in their shoes and try to understand why they are angry/sad/jealous. If they hit their younger sibling, for instance, let them know how their sibling may have felt and ask them what they might do to improve things next time. If they give you a heartfelt reason why they behaved badly (they might say, "You don't play with me anymore. You are always taking care of Daniel!") let them know you understand how difficult it must be not to have your full attention as they once did and ask them if they would like to join you on a mummy-daughter day doing something they love. Little by little, enlist their help taking care of younger siblings so they feel like they are playing an important role in the household.

THE BENEFITS OF UNCONDITIONAL LOVE

Author, poet, and children's advocate Laura Mulcha (UNICEF, 2021) recently undertook a fascinating set of interviews with leading experts to discover why love is so important for children. Her words, which are available online, highlight the many different reasons why unconditional love—loving your child "warts and all"— is so important.

Speaker Vikram Patel of Harvard Medical School, for instance, spoke of how mental health is our greatest personal asset and of how it impacts the way we think, feel, and behave. Loving children, being kind and patient with them, and helping them develop their emotional intelligence can help them lead happier, healthier, longer lives. Cornelius Williams, Associate Director and global Chief of Child Protection, UNICEF, spoke of matters from an economic standpoint. It is vital to protect children against violence, he argued, because it is the most useful investment we can make to improve the health, well-being, and productivity of societies. Dr. Bernadette Madrid, Director of the Child Protection Unit of the University of the Philippines Manila, argued for the importance of universal support for parents to break intergenerational cycles of anger, neglect, and abuse.

Unconditional love can sometimes be difficult to demonstrate. It definitely does not involve accepting everything your child does. On the contrary, it requires continuous work, endless patience, and a willingness to stick to a strategy you feel might work, even if it "failed" the first or second time around.

When you feel like throwing in the towel and taking a one-way flight to the Bahamas, take a breather. Remember that most behaviors that "drive you crazy" are developmentally normal. Your child is growing, learning, and experimenting; he or she is not "a finished product." The next time your toddler is running around incessantly and his older sibling is throwing toys across the room, remember the saying that when it comes to children, "The days go slowly but the years flyby."

As your child grows up, you will discover a wonderful, interesting human being you can start having fascinating conversations with, share interests, and take part in hobbies with. However, you will find yourself looking back at cute baby and toddler pictures of your kids and wishing you could relive those early days when your child had chubby cheeks, a toothless grin, and a love for you that made you feel like a hero. You can always be a figure to look up to for your child, for they will never stop needing you. When you treat them with love and respect, they will return these gifts wholeheartedly.

LOVE ARISES FROM UNDERSTANDING AND EMPATHY

It is very hard to make your children feel your love if you cannot demonstrate the quality of empathy.

Exercising empathy means taking the focus off yourself and putting it onto your child. Once you understand the essence of what your child is feeling, let them know it by helping them label their feelings (Dr. Joyce, n.d.).

Empathy breaks down barriers and stops heated conflicts in their tracks. It can be considered the essential first step toward sound conflict resolution, because it diffuses tension, puts people on an equal footing, and demonstrates a willingness to understand and help someone else. Empathy must be genuine if it is to bear fruit. If yours is half-hearted, self-interested, or inadequate, it will cause your child more harm than good as they may feel disappointed, unloved, and even confused.

It may be hard for you to show empathy for others if your parents did not share it with you. If so, you may struggle to love yourself and be very overwhelmed when you have to "deny yourself" to take on the pain of someone else. You may have spent much of your life suppressing pain, anger, and other difficult emotions and the raw emotion of your child may "block you up" inside. Therapy can be useful if you think that trauma or PTSD is stopping you from accessing your emotions and showing empathy. We mentioned the many ill-effects that abuse and anger can have on children and sometimes, the damage is deep and requires professional help to unravel. Don't be ashamed or let stigma, shame, or fear of judgment stand in your way. By working through your trauma, finding positive ways to deal with your pain, and learning to express yourself, you can gain the strength you need to be a more empathetic parent. In reality, working on your own mental health and well-being should be considered a brave, useful, wise investment in your child.

7

STAY A STEP AHEAD OF ANGER-INDUCING SITUATIONS

Despite improving your emotional regulation skills, you may find that on occasions, you still get angry—and that is okay because you are human and anger sometimes serves a good purpose. Anger is only problematic when it becomes derailed and hurts others, causes a breakdown in communication, or is harmful to one's own (or others') health.

Anger can be unproductive when it is suppressed. It can also become obsessive—when you feel slighted by someone repeatedly, it can result in hatred, triangulation with others, or a wish for vengeance. Suppressing your anger to avoid conflicts at all costs can result in passive-aggressive behavior that is painful to others because it manifests itself in sarcasm, sabotage or boycotting. It can also contribute to depression, anxiety, low self-esteem, and alcohol and substance abuse.

Aggressive anger is the flip side of the coin. It can cause direct mental and (sometimes) physical harm to property and of course, to people. People with classic passive-aggressive behaviors may be "yes persons" to their bosses and colleagues, agreeing to tasks they don't think they should be doing. They can simmer inside for days or weeks, only to have a big outburst one day, slamming the phone down or throwing their keyboard across the room and causing damage as well as a sense of fear and insecurity in their colleagues. Sometimes, they can take their work frustrations out on their family. In children, aggressive anger can manifest itself in the form of bullying and the destruction of school or personal property.

In both adults and children, improperly channeled anger can result in an inability to forgive—and this can mean that they end up carrying a burden all their lives. Forgiveness is liberation. As found in a Mayo Clinic study *(Mayo Clinic, 2008)* it is good for your health. Holding a grudge, on the contrary, affects the nervous and cardiovascular systems. In one study, people who focused on a grudge had a faster heart rate and elevated blood pressure. They also had a sense of loss of control and increased muscle tension. When they imagined forgiving someone, on the other hand, they felt more positive and calmed down and negative physiological changes dissipated. The researchers recommended:

- Acknowledging that you feel pain and anger when somebody hurts you or lets you down. Recognizing that healing does not happen passively; it requires change.

- Trying to empathize with the person who caused you pain or at least finding a motive or reason for the hurtful action. Sometimes they may not have meant to hurt you at all. They may be in pain themselves and they may have taken it out on you because they trust and feel comfortable with you. If you can, this is the time in which you can say, "I forgive you."

- Enjoying the mental freedom that comes with letting go of a grudge. At this stage, you may also be filled with compassion for others who have experienced the same hurt as you.

Even when you learn to forgive someone, new situations constantly arise that can make you feel unjustly treated. This is why knowing the causes of your anger and how to constructively resolve it, are key. Rely on the following tips to help you cope with anger:

▶ **Make your life simpler.** If you feel overwhelmed by the number of obligations pulling you in different directions, give up a few obligations so you don't have to deal with so many self-imposed triggers.

▶ **Work on your communication skills.** When someone says something you don't like or a situation becomes tense, don't react without thinking. Slow your thought process down and listen to others so you have a reasoned, realistic view of the situation.

▶ **Own your emotions.** Take a page out of the book of mindfulness and allow yourself to feel negative emotions like anger. Avoid repressing what you feel, since you can then become a prisoner to it.

▶ **Take time to care for yourself.** There are many useful, healthy ways to deal with anger and tackle stress proactively but most require time. Numerous studies have shown that holistic activities like yoga, tai chi, and mindfulness meditation, can all be powerful ways to pulverize stress. Regular exercise is also beneficial to your physical and mental health. Swedish scientists found (*Agudelo et al, 2014*) that physical exercise protects human beings against stress-induced depression. It does so by inducing changes in skeletal muscle that can help purge the blood of a substance that accumulates in blood when we are stressed and causes harm to the brain.

One of the best things about exercise is that it can reduce anxiety and stress even long after a workout is over. One study found (University of Maryland, 2012) for instance, that both exercise and quiet rest are equally effective at reducing anxiety levels initially. However, once people are emotionally stimulated for around 20 minutes, the stress levels of those who rested go back up while people who exercised maintain their lowered anxiety levels.

EMBRACING EMOTIONAL BALANCE AND HAPPINESS IN YOUR LIFE

Anger management does not merely involve exercising emotional regulation during a tense encounter. It requires the pursuit of a balanced, happy life—one that can act as an important buffer against life's many daily setbacks. When you feel satisfied with your work relationships and personal relationships, it can be easier to put conflicts into perspective. Having an imbalanced life, on the other hand, can cause you to focus (some- times obsessively) on the things that make you angry.

LIVING A HAPPIER LIFE

The first sentence of Tolstoy's *Anna Karenina* strikes a cord. It reads: "Happy families are all alike; every unhappy family is unhappy in its own way."

It is the same with individuals. Our fears, burdens, and sadness tend to be highly personal and particular, yet happiness usually involves the exercise of key strategies that are common to most emotionally intelligent people. These include:

- **Reframing Negative Thoughts into Positive Ones**

Emotionally intelligent people know how to convert a negative thought such as "I lost my job, I'll never find an equally good one," to "I've lost my job but I always thought it was time to branch out and try other areas of interest. In a way, this has inspired me to send my CV to companies I have always dreamed of working at."

- **Expressing Anger**

In previous chapters we went through the dangers of emotional suppression, indicating that it could lead to the adoption of unhealthy behaviors. Suppressed anger can only do two things: manifest itself in explosive anger or stay deep within, resulting in severe damage to your mental and physical health and well-being.

• SurroundingYourself with Positive People

Being around positive, emotionally available, emotionally intelligent people is contagious in the best possible way. People who have a winning attitude to life can teach you so many vital lessons about how to deal with disappointment. Motivational speaker, Jim Rohn once stated that people tend to assume many qualities of the five people they spend the most time with. If you are a busy person, why spend the little free time you have with people who will only bring you down and sap out the energy you are working so hard to maintain?

• Loving Yourself

Whitney Houston's song about the greatest love of all existing within yourself is almost a cliché but self-hatred brings nothing good to oneself or one's loved ones and acquaintances. You can't keep giving others your best self if you are stressed, tired, or frazzled. Be kind to yourself so you have the best chance of maintaining your calm during potentially triggering situations.

- **Avoiding Hate**

There is plenty of hatred in the world so don't bring more of it into your or other people's lives. Watch yourself when you are talking with loved ones or friends and using social media. Don't use chats or social media sites to vent frustration on others. Make a conscious effort to bring happiness and light to the people you interact with and try to bring peace and positivity to the world, one person at a time.

- **Feeding Your Body with the Fuel It Needs**

Aim to consume a healthy, Mediterranean-style diet, which is made up of healthy proteins, pulses, fruits and vegetables, and healthy Omega-3 essential fats. Research shows (Sanchez-Villegas et al, 2009) that this diet is linked to a lower chance of depression. The specific reasons for this phenomenon are unknown though researchers believe that it has something to do with the Mediterranean's diet's ability to fight inflammation, help prevent heart disease, repair oxygen-related cell damage, and more. Make sure to eat plenty of fiber as well, since it will help improve your gut health. Recent studies have shown there is a vital connection between the gut and the mind.

That is, there is a link between depression and having low levels of specific gut bacteria.

• Sleeping Seven to Nine Hours a Night

Adults should aim to get between seven and nine hours of sleep but in the U.S., one in three adults do not meet this goal (as reported by the CDC). When you lack sleep, you can become irritable, jumping at the slightest provocation. To be precise, one sleepless night can cause a 30% rise in emotional stress. A good night's sleep, on the other hand, helps to reset the anxious brain (Simon et al, 2019)—which is probably why Shakespeare's Macbeth called sleep the "balm of hurt minds."

• Having Good Friends

Communicating with friends reduces stress levels and keeps you grounded and connected. In this day and age, it is easy to keep up with friends from across the globe and there is always someone around to chat with at any time of the day. If it's been a while since you spoke to your best friend, suggest a video call, chat on Messenger, or better yet, make a date to meet up soon.

- **Wishing Good for Others**

Wishing the best for others helps to cool down tense situations, keeps the mind calm, induces positive feelings, and brings positive vibes right back at you. Research published in the *Journal of Happiness Studies*, for instance, has found that simply wishing someone the best can help lower anxiety and stress (Gentile et al, 2019). Researchers found that practicing loving-kindness boosts empathy and happiness and reduces anxiety while wishing others well improves one's sense of connectedness to others and sense of care.

- **Finding Meaningful Pastimes**

It is much easier to snap at small provocations when you feel empty or when there are few exciting things going on in your life. When you have a purposeful hobby that fulfils and excites you, it is much easier to feel positive and grateful and view conflicts within a wider perspective.

- **Avoiding News and Social Media Overdoses**

While staying abreast of important local, national, and international news is important for all people, obsessing about health scares and disasters can heighten your stress levels and can even trigger anxiety or depression.

Keep your social media use within reasonable bounds, since abusing this type of media is linked to increased depression and loneliness. One University of Arkansas study (Primack et al, 2021) showed that young adults who increased the amount of time spent on social media were significantly more likely to develop depression within six months.

IDENTIFYING AND UNDERSTANDING YOUR TRIGGERS

An emotional trigger can be anything—including a memory, a tone of voice, or a situation that makes you anxious. Identifying your personal triggers is important because once you know they usually get a reaction out of you, you can stop giving them the power to do so and begin to realize that you are actually in control of how you respond.

Common Triggers

Everyone has a unique set of triggers. Look through this list of common ones and ask yourself if any are pertinent to you or your child:

- Unjust treatment
- Abandonment

- Bad looks from others
- Friends or loved ones being distant when you need them
- Feeling helpless
- Attempts for others at manipulation or control over your life
- A challenge to your values or beliefs
- Judgment from others
- Criticism from others
- Fierce competition from others
- Being told what todo
- Sarcasm
- Feeling unloved or unwanted
- Rejection
- Being lied to
- Being betrayed
- Being ostracized or ignored
- Feeling like someone is trying to take up too much of your time
- A loss of independence

You will know that this or other events/sensations are triggers because your body and mind will have telltale reactions such as:

- A racing heartrate
- Taking in short, rapid breaths
- Feeling dizzy
- Trembling
- Perspiring (particularly in your palms)
- Digestive upset or a churning stomach
- Feeling agitated
- Facial flushing
- Tense neck and/or shoulder muscles
- Clenching yourjaw
- Forming a fist with your hands

ANALYZING YOUR REACTION TO TRIGGERS

In addition to manifesting physical signs of stress, what do you do when a trigger presents itself before you? Ask yourself vital questions to hone your self-awareness. Do you pursue others, trying to "force connection?" Do you buckle down and try to please your adversary? Do you try to blame someone else? Do you drink alcohol or take substances? Do you shut down and withdraw, leaving the place where the trigger occurred and refusing to discuss the matter with others? Do you get angry, throwing things around and shouting?

Try to understand why you usually pick a specific way or ways to react to triggers. Sometimes the connection is not immediately obvious. For instance, you may not like people who are overly competitive because you may have grown up with a sibling who was always challenging you in a negative way. People who are unavailable to you may trigger you because you are afraid of abandonment owing to a parent having passed away when you were young. Working out the causality of your triggers is one of the most challenging but rewarding components of good anger management because it is only when you address past and current hurts that you can stop triggers from manifesting themselves inappropriately.

OWNING YOUR EMOTIONS

Identify what you are feeling—sadness, anger, frustration, fear, disgust, and more, accepting them fully and knowing that they do not define your character. You may be feeling these emotions right now but they normally change, as does your perception of a person or situation. Remind yourself of past situations which may have provoked these emotions (perhaps you were afraid of flying or you found it very embarrassing to express your interest in someone). Think of how much you may have changed in time and understand that emotions are not permanent or definitive.

TAKING A BREAK AND REFRAMING TRIGGERING SITUATIONS

Once you have recognized and accepted your emotions, let your tension go. Breathe, have a small snack or beverage to fuel body and mind, go for a walk, touch things around you with a pleasant texture, or listen to an uplifting song. In this calmer state, look back at the situation and let empathy come to the forefront. Try to understand why your friend, colleague, or partner may have reacted less amicably than they normally would. Is there stress in their life? Were they recently reprimanded by their boss? Is someone important to them struggling against an illness? More often than not, people have good intentions and they don't set out to ruin your day, hurt you, or make you angry.

COMMUNICATING KINDLY WITH OTHERS

In this new, calmer state of mind, it is much easier to communicate your needs to others. If your colleague was short with you or they didn't answer a question with the detail you needed, wait until they are a little more receptive. Later in the day, when you are having a coffee break together, you can say something like, "Earlier I asked you when the deadline was for this task and I could tell you were really busy. It made me feel a little reluctant to approach you. Next time, if you're super busy, feel free to ask me to come back later because I do need that information but I'd rather return when you are able to explain it fully to me." The greatest likelihood (if they are reasonable, emotionally intelligent people) is that they will either apologize or explain why they snapped. At any rate, they will probably think twice before letting their stress out on you in the future.

INVESTING TIME IN YOUR HEALING JOURNEY

Although it can help to think of each trigger and analyze how you handled it, long-term healing is something that may involve identifying harmful relationship patterns, honing mindfulness, and journaling. For some people, it involves therapy. Specialists in relationship counseling can help you identify learned patterns of behavior that have led you to embark on unhealthy relationships, suppress anger, blow up when you're angry, and more.

Your therapist can also propose practical exercises that can enlighten you on the extent to which your beliefs can shape your reactions to conflict.

IDENTIFYING YOUR CHILD'S TRIGGERS

Your child may still be too young to identify their own triggers, observe their reactions to them, reframe situations, keep their eye on the ultimate goal, and communicate their needs. However, you are the perfect person to do so and as time passes and they mature, you can teach them all the emotional regulation skills you have learned along the way.

Knowing your child's triggers can also help you stop a situation before it gets out of hand. Keep in mind that the problem is not the trigger itself, but rather, the way your child perceives it. Some children might boil over and start screaming if they are told to do something they don't want to. Others may quietly accept your instructions but become silent and withdrawn, barely communicating with you out of a fear that you will spot something they haven't done or ask them to work harder at school or at home. As a parent, your job is to help them communicate their emotions effectively— which is why recognizing the signs that can set them off is so important.

Be observant as to the situations, times of day, people, tasks, hobbies, and other factors that seem to accompany your child's outbursts or withdrawal. For instance, you may find that every time your child plays a specific computer game, they get very frustrated because the game freezes up or has glitches. Your child may start acting up half an hour or so before bedtime because they want to spend more quality time with you. They may be moodier after school because of an argument they had with others or because they are having difficulties making friends. Observe their words as well as their body language and learn to "connect the dots." Children won't always be open about what is causing them pain or sadness so you need to be quite the detective and ask gentle questions that will encourage them to tell you more about their daily experiences. Other people in your life (grandparents, family friends, siblings) can also do their observatory work and give you information you may have missed, so don't under-take this task alone.

HELPING YOUR CHILD IDENTIFY THEIR TRIGGERS

As your child matures, they should also learn the pillars of emotional regulation, one of the most important of which is knowing what triggers them.

With younger children, it all begins by identifying and talking about feelings. Ask them what makes them sad, angry, or happy. They will learn to think back and analyze the effect that different situations, experiences, and people can have on them. Next, connect the dots for them. Explain, in simple words, how emotions and behavior are linked. Thus, you might say, "I notice that when you are tired, you start to cry." Show them that behavior has consequences and that eliminating triggers may require behavioral changes. In this example, for instance, napping at regular times and sleeping earlier will eliminate their trigger.

You should also teach children to recognize key physical signs and sensations caused by triggers. These include the effects listed above such as flushed cheeks, a warm sensation in the face, and a fast heartbeat. Children should know that these signs mean they are very close to losing their cool and that they can rely on a strategy that appeals to them to avoid an outburst.

Finally, teach your kids the art of cueing. Once they know how to label their emotions, focus on one emotion—for instance, sadness. Agree that you will use a specific cue (for instance, raising your right hand) when you notice your child is feeling this emotion.

This cue can serve as a sign that it is time for them to use their chosen calming strategy. If they need a little help, sit by their side, use a gentle touch and calming words, and try to lead them through their chosen activity— which could be a progressive muscle relaxation or breathing exercise. This strategy may take several tries to perfect but rest assured that you will eventually help your child know themselves better, improve their emotional regulation skills, and feel more confident about their abilities to negotiate challenges and stressors successfully.

DON'T MINIMIZE OR ENGAGE WITH YOUR CHILD'S ANGER

One of the most bothersome things that can happen when anyone is angry, is for someone to tell them they are overacting, making a mountain out of a molehill, or being weak. These words hurt your children just as much, if not more, so make sure you validate their feelings when they are upset.

Don't react to their anger, either. Instead, encourage them to differentiate between how they feel (their emotion) and how they act (their behavior). For instance, they should know that it is fine to feel angry that their little sibling threw their ice-cream to the ground but that it is not acceptable (or fruitful) to hit their sibling or have a tantrum. Give them all the time they need to talk about their feelings and teach them how to handle these emotions. Let them know that it is never bad to feel anxious, scared, sad, angry, and other emotions. Teach them important emotional regulation techniques so they know that they have a choice in how they handle all good and bad emotions. Important steps to take include:

TEACHING KIDS COPING STRATEGIES

We have highlighted the importance of teaching children to label their emotions, discover their triggers, and try to understand the reasons why specific situations bother them. Once children are confident with these tasks, they can find new ways to channel negative energy. Each child will have his or her own preferred methods, which can include telling themselves positive things, like "I am okay," "I am in control of my emotions," and "I am strong."

SHOWING CHILDREN THAT THEY HAVE POWER OVER THEIR EMOTIONS

Your children should know that the actions they take can help them feel more or less in control of their emotions. For instance, they can learn that by raising their voice, they can feel more stressed and angry. On the other hand, by counting to 10 and breathing, they can enter a much calmer state—one in which they feel in control of their emotions, not vice-versa.

GIVING CHILDREN CONSEQUENCES FOR THEIR ACTIONS

If a child does something inappropriate (like hit a sibling) they should have a consequence or punishment. Let them know you are not punishing them for their emotion (anger), but rather, for their action (hitting).

NOT BEING A PUSHOVER

Just because your child tells you that they are sad or angry does not mean they should get away with evading chores, homework, or other character-building tasks.

CREATING A LIST OF SOLUTIONS AND A GOOD ESCAPE PLAN

Have a list of strategies and tools that tend to work well with your child. Include the compromises both you and your child may have made and find out how to give your child what they actually want, not what they superficially desire. Work out your own needs as well and express these to them in a way your kids understand. By sharing your emotions, children are more likely to take a cooperative, non-defensive stance.

Have a trusty escape plan you can use during particularly tough days. This may involve going for a run, calling your mom, or having a relaxing bath. You don't always have to solve conflicts in the present moment. Letting a little time pass can help you and your child reach a state in which both of you are more willing to compromise to come to a fruitful solution.

GIVING YOUR CHILD THE GIFT OF FREE TIME

Cultivate a relaxing presence and your child will do the same. Being stable and reliable can help both of you progress in the same direction, away from anger. You need to unwind after a hard day but so do your children. Moreover, they need to start learning the value of self-kindness and decompression from a young age so they keep these healthy habits up when they are older.

Don't feel the obligation to enroll your child in every extra-curricular activity possible. Pay heed to the words of Kathy Hirsh-Pasek, PhD, co-author of Einstein Never Used Flashcards: How Our Children Really Lear— And Why They Need to Play More and Memorize Less.

She emphasizes the importance of allowing kids to just "be" and even "waste time" if they need to. When kids have nothing to do, they indulge in fantasy play, learn to manage their time, read, observe, investigate, and discover talents and interests that lay hidden when their schedules are too full.

EMBRACING NATURAL RELAXATION METHODS

When it comes to proactive stress-busting strategies, study after study has shown (Creswell et al, 2014) that mind-body activities such as meditation, yoga, and controlled breathing are among the most effective. Scientists have discovered that taking part in a brief mindfulness session for three consecutive days lowers stress and strengthens psychological stress resilience.

One study *(Buric et al, 2017)* found that mind-body interventions like yoga, tai chi, and meditation don't simply relax people; they also reverse the molecular reactions in our DNA which cause poor health and depression.

Another simple yet powerful habit to adopt is to spend time in nature. Living near a green area, spending a few minutes in a nature-filled spot, and even having plants at home can help you feel calmer.

For something fun you can try out with kids, head to the woods and enjoy a "forest bath." The latter simply involves opening all your senses—sights, sound, touch, and even taste—to the beauty around you. Ask children to notice the lovely sound that autumn leaves make under their feet, the beauty of mushrooms growing in clusters, or the graceful song of birds.

DON'T FORGET TO HAVE FUN WITH YOUR KIDS

Time really does fly with your kids and as your child enters the pre-teen and teen years, you sometimes begin to wish you had worried less about being "perfect" and simply had more fun with them. The good news is that it is never too late to create beautiful memories centered around simply being together and having a good time. Be imaginative and open yourself up to spontaneous opportunities to share your child's interests with them. If they are enterprising and want to start a lemonade stand in the summer, for instance, why not head to the store together to purchase all the ingredients they need, plus a few cute accessories such as swizzle sticks and cute glasses that will help them attract "customers"?

Why not take surprise excursions (think an ad hoc picnic, a day at the beach, a mani-pedi, experience an escape room activity for the family, and the like) once in a while? Ask your kids to make their own bucket list of activities. When you have a free morning, afternoon, or day, pick an activity from their lists and show them how much fun saying "yes" to unexpected opportunities can be.

CONCLUSION

One of the most detrimental opinions on anger is that it is a "bad" thing that is always accompanied by aggression, shouting, and abuse. Anger is no worse than happiness, sadness, fear, shame, and guilt. It is a basic human emotion and, like all other emotions, it can be expressed either effectively or ineffectively.

In earlier chapters, we highlighted how beneficial anger can be. Anger is a sign that change is necessary if you are to progress as a parent and human being. It can arise when you are too giving and others abuse your kindness, when you keep emotions bottled inside, or when you are not accustomed to assertively expressing your limits to others.

Managing anger effectively toward children is, above all, a project that involves work on oneself. It starts off with being aware of the things that can trigger your anger, noticing the sometimes-subtle signs that you are reaching the end of your tether, and identifying the situations and/or people that interfere with your ability to stay calm.

Anger is an opportunity to know yourself better; to think back to your childhood and try to understand why you adopt certain patterns of behavior when tense situations arise. Some people seek to resolve conflicts quickly; others need a little time alone. Some have a tendency to involve third parties in damaging triangles.

To hone your emotional intelligence, you need to take a step back and be an observer of your past and present. Think of how you felt as a child and what strategies your parents used to express their anger. If they screamed, punished you, or sent you away without trying to understand the causes of your behavior, it can be easy to find yourself falling into the same trap when you become a parent.

If you are reading this book, it is a sign that you are aware of the dangers of uncontrolled anger. In earlier chapters, we presented various studies showing the many detrimental effects that aggressive behavior can have on children.

These effects are long-term and they affect children's physical and mental health. Some can even shorten their lifespan or affect their mental well-being. Others can make it harder for them to form healthy relationships with others.

Knowing your triggers and identifying your own emotions are the first steps toward helping your child regulate theirs. There are many strategies you can try, one of which involves working on your life as a whole, looking for any imbalances that need addressing, being kinder to yourself, giving yourself a break, and trying out tried-and-tested stress-busting activities like yoga, mindfulness meditation, and time spent in nature.

If you suspect anxiety or depression may be making matters worse, or your outbursts are strong and/or frequent, it is important to seek help from a professional therapist. Approaches such as cognitive behavioral therapy can help you understand the vital link between your thoughts, emotions, and behaviors, and you will be guided through a series of practical exercises that will help you find more effective outlets for anger.

When you make a change in your own behavior, your children won't necessarily follow suit immediately but you will be doing more good than you can imagine by modeling positive behaviors. From the time children are very young, they can learn some of the techniques you find successful. These can include identifying and labeling emotions, finding out their cause, exercising empathy toward others, brainstorming solutions, and choosing one or more strategies to try out next time.

"Keeping your eye on the prize" is important throughout your learning process and experimentation with the strategies you have learned. When conflict arises with others, even if you disagree with the values and beliefs they are espousing, focus on how valuable your relationship is. Learn to "choose your battles" and see conflict as an opportunity to exercise your best teamwork skills. Conflict is not a shouting match or a battle of wills. It is a crucial opportunity for you and your children to understand each other better; to grasp each other's complexities, mysteries, and fears; and to utilize this information to become more patient and understanding with each other.

On some days, you will feel on top of the anger game. On other days, you may feel like anger has got the better of you. If so, turn to love—it is a powerful emotion and a fundamental human need. When you feel angry at your child, remember that they have as great a need for love and understanding as you do.

Sometimes you will need a little "me time" to feel restored and reinvigorated. At other times, a surprise family getaway will mend bridges and remind everyone that despite occasional conflicts, you are all pretty cool. When you feel stressed, your workload is too large, or you are overcoming tough losses, cut yourself some slack. Give yourself a day off to relax, soothe pain, and keep stress down through healthy activities that your child can also try out.

Prioritize self-compassion and your child will do the same. Parents sometimes play the "comparing game"—one that can cause pain and anguish to yourself and your child. Comparing ourselves with others stops when we realize that often, our greatest weaknesses are also our strengths. Our passion, drive, and commitment can result in anger when we feel that we have "failed," but it can inspire us to make positive changes for ourselves and others.

On days when you feel like "throwing in the towel," remember that one bad day does not define you; nor does it define your child. Try to recall a time in your childhood when your parents handled your emotions with empathy, helping you to understand others and encouraging you to value these relationships—even when conflicts arose.

If you had a tough childhood and parental support was scarce, take solace in those moments when an adult supported you, understood you, and tried to be a positive role model.

Childhood flies by. Once your children leave home, they carry the tools you have given them. You cannot shield them from stress, pain, or disappointment but you can teach them how to create meaningful bonds with others, negotiate conflicts successfully, and find purpose from life's toughest lessons.

Show Others How to Choose the Best Possible Outcome When They Feel Overwhelmed By Anger

You now know all the strategies you need to be a calm yet assertive parent who sets firm boundaries but enforces them with kindness and understanding.

Simply by leaving your honest opinion of this book on Amazon, you'll show other people that anger is a normal human emotion that can be used to make vital changes within the family dynamic. You will help them hone the knowledge, skills, and essential strategies they need to establish healthy family patterns that their children can pass along to future generations.

Scan to leave feedback or Stars:

A FREE GIFT FOR MY READERS!

Included with your purchase of this book is your free copyof
Kids and Electronics
9 practical strategies to help you manage and limit your children's screen use

Scan the QR code below to receive your free copy:

If you loved *"Anger Management for Parents"*, you might also love Vivian's other book:

Parenting a child with ADHD doesn't have to be a rollercoaster ride.

By following the guidance and applying the program in this book, you will be able to:

- Raise your child without the unnecessary frustrations.
- **Know how to proceed towards diagnosis,** which professional to choose, and which medication is right for your child (if any!).
- **Anticipate what to expect** in each stage of your child's growth from preschool to adolescence.
- Find out how to help your child with their peer problems and **boost their academic development.**
- Be aware of ways to handle environmental stimuli and **avoid the triggers** that send your child on a rampage.
- **Also take care of yourself** to stay healthy and fully present for your child with ADHD, as well as your entire family.

AND SO MUCH MORE...

FOLLOW THE 8-STEP PROGRAM TO EMPOWER YOUR CHILD...

Including ideas for games and activities to nurture your kid's ability to adapt, cope and thrive.

Scan Me

Made in the USA
Monee, IL
08 May 2024

58166298R00114